How the Light Gets In
& Other Headlong Epiphanies

Brian Doyle

ORBIS BOOKS
Maryknoll, New York 10545

ORBIS BOOKS
Maryknoll, New York 10545

Founded in 1970, Orbis Books endeavors to publish works that enlighten the mind, nourish the spirit, and challenge the conscience. The publishing arm of the Maryknoll Fathers and Brothers, Orbis seeks to explore the global dimensions of the Christian faith and mission, to invite dialogue with diverse cultures and religious traditions, and to serve the cause of reconciliation and peace. The books published reflect the views of their authors and do not represent the official position of the Maryknoll Society. To learn more about Maryknoll and Orbis Books, please visit our website at www.maryknollsociety.org.

Library of Congress Cataloging-in-Publication Data
Doyle, Brian, 1956 November 6-
  [Poems. Selections]
  How the light gets in & other headlong epiphanies / by Brian Doyle.
    pages ; cm
  ISBN 978-1-62698-145-4 (pbk.)
    I. Title.
PS3604.O9547A6 2015
811'.6--dc23

2015010626

Thank God, though I know what is going on,
I don't understand a single thing.
—*Wystan Hugh Auden*

There is a crack in everything/
That's how the light gets in.
—*Leonard Cohen*

The Lord GOD hath given me the tongue . . .
that I should know how to speak a word in season to him
that is weary . . . he wakeneth mine ear to hear.
—*Isaiah 50: 4-5*

To pay attention, this is our endless and proper work.
—*Mary Oliver*

To David James Duncan,
with heartfelt thanks for years
of kindness and wit and laughter

Thanks & Etc.

Most of these poems, or "proems," appeared in *The Christian Century, First Things,* and *U.S. Catholic* magazines, and I am especially thankful to Jill Peláez Baumgaertner, Paul Lake, and Cathy O'Connell-Cahill, respectively, for not moaning overmuch when their mailboxes filled with these odd songs. Thanks too to Christopher Cahill at *The Recorder,* the lovely journal of the American Irish Historical Society; to Phillip Harvey at *Eureka Street* in Australia (eurekastreet.com.au); to Claire Columbo at *Theopoetics* (theopoetics.org); and to Brad Modlin at the excellent journal *Quarter After Eight,* at Ohio University, who asked me to riff on a line from the poet Charles Baudelaire, which explains, a bit, the poem "Life is a Hospital in Which Every Patient Is Haunted by the Desire to Change Beds," a line from Baudelaire's *Paris Spleen.*

Finally my thanks to my cheerful brilliant friend the Reverend Bill Harper, freshly retired from Grace Church on Bainbridge Island, Washington, for letting me publish the poem about him; I report with pleasure that the surgery was successful, and that Bill is once again an entertaining bolt of headlong spiritual energy loose in this blessed world. That man has Wendell Berry tattooed *on his forearms,* so he reads a great American poet all day every day, and every time he waves hello to someone, a Wendell Berry poem waves in the air like a gentle bright flag; how cool is that?

Also by Brian Doyle

Novels
Martin Martin • *The Plover*
Mink River • *Cat's Foot*

Short Stories
Bin Laden's Bald Spot & Other Stories

Poems
A Shimmer of Something
Thirsty for the Joy: Australian & American Voices
Epiphanies & Elegies

Nonfiction
*The Grail: A Year Ambling & Shambling Through an
Oregon Vineyard in Pursuit of the Best Pinot Noir in the Whole Wild World*
The Wet Engine: Exploring the Mad Wild Miracle of the Heart

Essay Collections
So Very Much the Best of Us • *A Book of Uncommon Prayer*
Children & Other Wild Animals • *Grace Notes*
The Thorny Grace of It • *Leaping: Revelations & Epiphanies*
Spirited Men • *Credo*
Saints Passionate & Peculiar • *Two Voices* (with Jim Doyle)

Contents

Poem for Your Wife
After Years of Marriage

Here is what I would like to say to you
That I never say to you, because I can't
Find the words, but I'm going to burble
Along here and hope for the best today.
There's no reason we should be in love,
And there are eleventy reasons why we
Should have run out of energy long ago.
I think maybe because we just stumbled
Into each other is why we are interested,
You know what I mean? I think we will
Maybe never get to the end of things to
Learn about the other; the first of which
Is whatever you think you know for sure
You don't, and the next is that when you
Think you have come to the end of stuff
To discover, you haven't, not in the least.
And your mere biographical information
Is the least engaging of all, other than the
Hilarious panoply of previous applicants;
It's the subtle daily and monthly opening,
The almost unnoticeable growing, a quiet
Letting-go of some things and acquisition
Of new things, that makes you essentially
A slightly different person every morning,
Which is riveting—and to be honest, sexy.
So there's that. Also making you laugh is

Endlessly entertaining. And we have kids,
But that one I have to pin on you: *I* didn't
Emit anyone from my nether private parts.
But I am grateful that *you* did—well done.

There Now Then

Or here's a particularly Australian moment, somehow,
It seems to me. I was shambling past a park in Sydney,
And I stopped to watch a few kids playing cricket, and
When they took a break I got to talking to this one boy
Who was interested that I was from America and knew
Nothing hardly about cricket, except that Bradman was
Inarguably The Best Player Ever, a most alluring phrase
We savor in America for Michael Jordan and Babe Ruth,
And the boy says to me *Here sir, step in and swing a bit,*
And I explain that I am old and busted and cannot do so,
And then there was a quintessentially Australian instant;
The boy, rather than giving up, says that *he'll* bat for *me.*
He lets a couple go wide—*You're just getting your eye!,*
He says—and then he hits for one, and then he *hammers*
A ball deep deep to what I would think of as center field.
You crushed that one, sir! he says to me, laughing. Now,
This was an adventure of all of nine minutes, some years
Ago, but it stays with me for all sorts of reasons, like the
Cheerful open grace and humor of the boy, which maybe
Are national virtues, and then the whirl of startled parrots
Arrowing out of the faraway gum trees as the ball arrived.
I walked on, sure I did, all the way to this almost last line,
But isn't it amazing how you are with me there now then?

The Under of Things

Young man asks me a question this morning:
Challenging question, challenging young guy,
Seemingly confrontational but not really, you
Know? The kind of young man who wears his
Challenging attitude like a proud jacket. *He* is
Not going to accept glittery pap from the Man.
But you can see the shy and a little frightened
Kid under the chippy attitude. The *suburbs*, he
Says, and there's a smear of sneer on the word.
You've lived there *all* your life? I want to snap
At him, sure I do. I'd like to say something tart
About how sneering's easy and attentiveness is
Hard and humility is hardest. But instead I find
Myself going on about how my kids knew fifty
Other kids, and how there are owls burbling out
Back every night in the firs, and how a neighbor
Lends his tools to everyone without a word, and
How we all quietly keep an eye on troubled folk
To be sure no one hassles them or steals or beats
Them, and how labels do not define the under of
Things, where people really live, and try to savor
And care for those they love, and not get shot at,
And put food on the table. Isn't that where all of
Us live, or want to? To my surprise and pleasure,
The young man suddenly bows, and we all laugh

At his grace. Later I tell him I wish I was as bold
In chippy questioning and abashed apology when
I was his age—I was only good at the former, but
I have been trying to work on the latter ever since.

October 27

You know what I remember first about my daughter being born?
Weirdly, not the miracle of it, or the bruised tender extraordinary
Courage of my wife, or the eerie alien glare of the birthing room,
Or the cheerful doctor chatting amiably as she hauled out our girl,
But my daughter staring at me, from the first instant she emerged.
She saw me and just stared and I was staring too, and we did that
For quite a long time, as I remember. The nurse hustled her off to
Be washed and I hustled over to keep our stares locked. I thought
Somehow that if our stares broke a crucial thing would be broken
And I couldn't stand that thought. I kept thinking we'd never met,
Formally, but we just could not stop staring. God knows what she
Thought. Me, I thought that she looked shockingly self-possessed
For someone who had just gone through a birth canal. That surely
Must have been a strenuous experience but she seemed essentially
Calm about the whole project. I couldn't read her expression at all.
She didn't appear rattled, or curious, or startled, or upset, or angry;
She just stared, like she was coolly examining me. Huge dark eyes.
Believe me I have seen that stare untold times since, and just about
Every time she fixed it on me, even when matters were tumultuous
Or worse, the obscure part of me that remembers everything woke
And shouted *o my god there it is again, just as it was the first time!*

Grátia Pléna

In the school playground in the woods at the coast in summer
I am praying the rosary using everything as beads. Hail raven
Full of grace the Lord is with thee. He was also once gawking
And perfect and croaked and mewed and those who heard him
Grinned at the piping of this rough new stammer of a creature.
Blessed art thou thimbleberry and last salmonberries and crow,
The blackberry clans, the nervous young doe. The fruit of such
An unimaginable inexhaustible womb. The robin so concerned
With good posture, the damselfly who silently says a new thing
About the color blue, the furred moths, the swerve of swallows.
Dóminus técum, brothers and sisters. The Lord is with thee, yes,
And with the boy with the baseball and the girl in the tall prayer
Of the grass, and the other boy clonking rocks and shouting hey,
Crawdads! The Lord is with them, in them, from them, all of us,
All of it, now; we have to remember to forget so as to remember.

What Do Poems *Do*?

I was, no kidding, a visiting writer in a *kindergarten* recently,
And the children asked me many wry and hilarious questions,
Among them *is that your real nose?* and *can you write a book
About a ruffed grouse, please?* But the one that pops back into
My mind this morning was *what do poems do?* Answers: swirl
Leaves along sidewalks suddenly when there is no wind. Open
Recalcitrant jars of honey. Be huckleberries in earliest January,
When berries are only a shivering idea on a bush. Be your dad
For a moment again, tall and amused and smelling like Sunday.
Be the awful wheeze of a kid with the flu. Remind you of what
You didn't ever forget but only mislaid or misfiled. Be badgers,
Meteor showers, falcons, prayers, sneers, mayors, confessionals.
They are built to slide into you sideways. You have poetry slots
Where your gills used to be, when you lived inside your mother.
If you hold a poem right you can go back there. Find the handle.
Take a skitter of words and speak gently to them, and you'll see.

The Way to Teach a Son How to Tie a Necktie

Is to stand behind him in front of a mirror and very slowly
Go through the ancient silly ritual: prop up the shirt collar,
Drape the tie around the holy squirming lean beloved neck
You have seen every day for years and years since the first
Moment you saw it peer out of its moist miraculous cavern.
Match the ends of the tie so that you don't have it drooping
Toward your knees, or the thinner end longer than the thick.
Why in heaven's name that matters is not a question we can
Answer in any sensible way; it just is. That's how my father
Taught me and his father him and so on back to Cúchulainn,
From whom we are descended for untold tens of generations.
No, the chances are slim that Cúchulainn wore a necktie. Do
Not ask me why he did not have to and we do. Then the first
Wrap, and then under, and then the other one through. Foxes
Chasing rabbits, see? No, rabbits do not wear neckties, that I
Know about, although maybe they do on dignified occasions
Like this one. Then you very gently pull the knot tight—very
Gently, see, while fiddling generally to let the knot look cool.
Why do we voluntarily strangle ourselves with useless cloth?
An excellent question. Neckties are like bright feathers, good
Only for preening. Some men use them to tell you where they
Went to college, or what clubs and tribes they belong to. Yes,
Neckties are like bumper stickers on cars sometimes. Exactly
So. Now we examine ourselves in the mirror: two beautifully
Dressed men, are we not? You remember this moment. There
Will be a moment like this for you someday, when you stand

Behind your son at the mirror and help him tie his tie and you
Will feel the same rush of love and memory and sadness, that
Time eats holy moments like this. My dad stood behind me at
The mirror. It was the day of his brother's wedding. Long ago
But yesterday and I remember he was tall and smiling and our
Ties matched. Do ties make sense? Only for that; only for this.

Three in the Morning

I do not think we talk enough about how every one of us
Has shuffled around the house in the middle of the night
Worried about voices raised downstairs, or a light on that
Shouldn't be, or someone crying softly. We walk around
Uncomfortably. We can't stay in bed but we can't fix the
Problem, for whatever reason. Sometimes your partner is
Better at soothing. Sometimes the pain will exhaust itself
If you leave it alone down there. Sometimes there is zero
To be done except shuffle around wearily. We test a lock,
Make sure there's coffee for tomorrow, check to see if an
Owl is sitting on the roof of the porch. Sometimes I draw
The moon if it's a riveting sliver. There's no good reason
To ever be up at this time. Nothing good happens at three
In the morning, unless you are going fishing before dawn.
I suppose we are all going fishing if we are up at that hour.

Nests Are So Brave and Awkward

Our daughter was released from the ward on Monday,
Just a lovely day, crisp and dry after a moist weekend,
And I showed her the lean subtle nest in the cedar tree.
Bushtits, those tiny eager verbs, stitched a long hirsute
Nest among hanging fronds with such astounding skill
That you would think it just detritus if you saw it at all.
We gaped at it for a while. The birds were a bit uneasy,
But no one was upset, and then my daughter went back
Inside, and soon was sick again, and then it was a crisis
Again, and so here I am out under the cedar. The crows
Across the street, I notice, will fly loudly past their nest
And then sort of sneak back to it with their construction
Materials. This seems funny to me somehow. I suppose
I could stand here for a year and never get to the end of
All the cool things going on. I am terrified. Nests are so
Brave and awkward. Everything I knew I knew I do not.
We want to say *she's better* so bad we practice saying it,
But then we can't say it. It was cool to stand by the tits'
Nest for a moment. It looks like the beard of an old man,
If the guy never had the energy or inclination to comb it.
Maybe he was weary, or he had lost a child or something
Like that—something that could make him totally forget.

At Four in the Afternoon
on a Hot Summer Day

Given the incalculable number of things that can go wrong today
And probably will, if you want to play the sure and certain odds,
Isn't it amazing that right this instant there is a hawk, and no one
Is shooting at it, or at you, and below the hawk is a grinning river,
And for one holy moment you get to see such a profligacy of gift,
And for this instant there is no logic, and reasoning, and thinking,
Just the hawk like a russet angel, and the shimmering of the river?

Oileán Acla

On Achill Island, the Island of Eagles off the shores of Ireland,
Before a coffin is carried to the cemetery, it rests a bit on chairs
Or sawhorses before the front door of the house of the departed.
People stand around and have a drink and tell stories. When it's
Time to carry the deceased to the grave, men pick up the casket,
And then kick out the chairs. That is how it is done in that place.
People have lived on Achill island for maybe six thousand years.
It's a small thing, the kicking out of the chairs, but that is how it
Is done in that place, and that is how it has always been done; to
Do a thing in a certain way in a certain place is a very fine thing,
It seems to me. That is what partly what places are made of, yes?
Things done in that way? Which is to say people saying that this
Is how we are who we are. Things change, sure they do, and yes,
Someday men will not kick over the chairs as they carry a friend
To his grave. But they did and they do and that is very fine thing.

At the Wake

At the wake I am standing in a corner near the whiskey table
When I overhear a snippet of conversation that delights me.
Referring to the deceased, a burly comic gentle man aged 52,
One man says to another One time we had a raving argument
About something or other—I can't remember what now. But
We were furious with each other and I stomped away. Could
Be I swore I would never talk to such a dork again. Next day
Life happens and I had to borrow his truck. Not only does he
Bring the truck but he helps me load and unload stuff. I think
We could just tell that story and cover the bases with Tommy,
You know what I mean? I bet every other guy here borrowed
That truck too, and probably every time Tommy came with it.
What else do you need to say about the man cooler than that?

Poem in Memory of
Tòmas Ó hArrachtáin

For a moment, at the funeral, as the gifts were being brought
Up the aisle by the nieces and nephews, and we all sat a little
Dazed at the fact that this was actually inarguably *happening*,
And that the wry beloved bachelor uncle was in the pine box
Toward which the nieces and nephews were sailing raggedly,
I stared down at all the shoes and boots I could see before me.
People had worn their good shoes, of course, all of them dark,
But it was the way they were ever so gently worn that riveted
Me for a while. The scuffed heel, the soles worn more on one
Side than the other, perhaps indicating pigeon-toes. One older
Man had one heel twice as thick as the other. One man's shoe
Had a heel so new it gleamed; the word *cobbler* came to mind,
And for an instant I could see standing in the library in the old
Home where the uncle had been a child, and chatting with him
About cobblers and awls and such, the uncle being a ferocious
Reader and a man of wide curiosity, and wondering do people
Even *go* to a cobbler anymore, is that now a dying profession?
And him saying something about cobblers' shops in the Béarra
Where his people anciently were from, and then recharging our
Whiskies, but then I remembered he was in a box, so that when
Later I stood by the bookcase in the old house, it was with Tom
Only in memory, which is thin as the wind compared to himself.

The Smokers' Corner

Recently I was in a city by a tremendous lake and was as usual
Wandering around on foot trying to get a sense of the geometry
And vocabulary of the place, how people and animals and trees
And plants staked claims and set up camp in this particular spot,
And I noticed, as if for the first time, all the quiet little smokers'
Corners in alleys and in places out of the wind and under bridge
Overpasses and in the huddles of bus shelters. Mostly they were
Neat, the smoking corners, with butt-buckets filled with sand, or
Ingenious devices designed for the disposal of tobaccan detritus.
And usually there were a couple of lawn chairs, or a picnic table.
After a while I started looking for them and I found them behind
Buildings and around the scraps of undefined lots between stores.
It was like once I started looking for them, they tiptoed out shyly
To say hey. You wouldn't believe how many I saw. Easily thirty.
For a long time I thought that smokers' corners were sad huddles
Where bedraggled half-junkies hurriedly inhaled their nico-candy,
And I would think how fast culture changes, and how when I was
A child *everyone* smoked and now there are only a few last exiles,
If you don't count young people for whom smoking is advertising
Something that they want you to think about how they seem to be.
But by the time I finished my wandering through this lakeside city
I realized these corners were actually tiny villages—almost chapels,
Places where two or more gathered and chatted and offered flame.
There was sacrifice of a sort, and ritual, and set customs and habits,
And the ceremonial torching of something that had been harvested
From the profligate soil. There was even something like abasement
As the smokers joked at their common predicament, their shunning

By the majority, which leads to rough camaraderie among the tribe
Of burners. To be honest, as I sat in one of the ratty old lawn chairs
For a moment to catch a rare shimmer of sun in the reluctant spring,
I felt a sudden affection for them, always being sent beyond the city
Walls to conduct themselves in a way they can't or won't relinquish;
There are so very many such corners, as you and I know all too well.

That's the Thing to Remember

Consider this, and then tell me what it is we must do.
A girl is born without arms and legs. She has a head.
The nurse washes and wraps her tenderly, and hands
Her to her mother; but the mother recoils. The father
Is called from the other room. He recoils too; he says
This is not what God wants and there's been an error
And they will not accept the child. He says the word
Blob. The poor man, says the nurse to me later. He's
Just totally rattled and lost his head. It's easy to snarl
At them but probably it's better to remember they're
Just completely shocked and exhausted. The girl was
Adopted by another nurse. She lived to be about four,
The girl. Sweet kid. What a laugh. The nurse and her
Husband, now, after the girl died, they adopted more
Kids. There really *are* couples like that on this planet.
That's the thing to remember. It's easy to be enraged,
I know. I have been furious plenty of times. But then
I think of the folks who thought that kid was the best
Gift *ever.* There's people like that on the planet, see?

Poem Exploring the Many Conceivable Reasons Why the Dog, Curled in His Chair, Occasionally Heaves a Huge Melodramatic Gargantuan Sigh

He is weary of the weight of his daily duties and responsibilities,
And is harking back to the headlong misadventures of his youth.

He is struck by a sudden miasma about the state of the biosphere,
And worries about the future of his beloved teenage housemates.

Having pondered the state of American literature today, he finds
That he cannot think of anyone nearly as good as Samuel Clemens.

Contemplating modern American politics, he confronts a plethora
Of lies, shrieks, rage, incitement to violence, and willful ignorance.

While slowly emerging from a pleasant nap, he realizes that he has
Not eaten a delicious mole or squirrel in days, and that he is aging.

He has realized suddenly that Peter Matthiessen is dead, and so our
Nation and world is reduced, and that wry clarion voice is no more.

He remembers that as a pup he was abandoned in the deepest forest,
And for an instant recalls the scent of wild dense green spring there.

He realizes that he will never pull a sled in the snows of the Yukon,
Or be a heroic hunter of rabbits in the islands of his ancestral Spain.

He thinks that the shaggy man in the room with him seems addicted
To the basketball game on television, while a *good* human teammate

Would stand up and bring him a gobbet of redolent crushed squirrel,
Or something along the mole line. But no—therefore, ergo, the Sigh.

In the Playground

I find the usual delights, like swings crowded with shrieking kids
And knots of mothers herding toddlers and two burly dads happily
Hitting ground balls and shouting complicated advice at tiny boys,
And basketball baskets with the two raggiest nets I have ever seen,
But then I see the United States of America painted on the cement,
And my mind flips and I am standing with my small daughter who
Jumps from Oregon all the way to *Utah*, dad! And then one terrific
Vault to *Oklahoma* which good thing it has a *handle* for me to land
On, dad! We spent a million hours in the United States in a shining
Wet playground near a river near the sea, me calling out the perfect
Names of the states as her sneakers landed on them, and her singing
Them, and me proud and moved, and her asking stories about them,
And me saying See how Michigan is a boxing glove, and California
Is a long hand cupping most of the West, and Alaska is twice Texas,
And let's stand together inside our lovely Oregon, there's just room
Enough here for all four of our feet, isn't this the coolest state *ever?*

At the Breakfast Table on a Thursday

There's a moment, while we read the newspaper
In the morning, when you are utterly completely
Absorbed by your section (news), and you reach
For your coffee, without looking, and your hand
Knows the general coordinates, but not the exact
Specific global position, and I watch with a deep
And abiding pleasure. I can see half of your face,
With your glasses half down your nose, and your
Wild and abundant cascade of hair, and a slice of
Those oceanic eyes, and the flapping wing of the
Newspaper, and your hand is exploring, and it all
Just seems so amazing to me. Every morning is a
Miracle all over again. The hand, the cup, the girl
Behind the sail of the paper, the cedar tree staring
In the window, the children asleep, the shape and
Manner of heaven patent and evident and as open
And accessible as the broad sky of the newspaper.

The Poem About What It's About

Here's my question. What if there was a poem
That didn't know what it was about until it got
To the end of itself? So that the poet's job isn't
To play with imagery and cadence and metrical
Toys in order to make a point, but rather to just
Keep going in order to find out that the poem is
About how hard it is to watch your kids get hurt
By things they can't manage and you cannot fix.
If *I* had been the boss of this poem I would have
Made it so they *can* manage things, or I could be
The quiet fixer I always wanted to be as a father;
But that's not what the poem wanted to be about,
It turns out. This poem is just like your daughter:
No one knows what's going to happen, and there
Will be pain, and you can't fix everything, and it
Hurts to watch, and you are terrified even as you
Try to stay calm and cool and pretend to manage.
Some poems you can leave when they thrash too
Much but kids are not those sorts of poems. They
Have to keep writing themselves, and it turns out
You are not allowed to edit. You're not in charge
At *all*—a major bummer. I guess there's a lesson
Here about literature, about how you have to sing
Without knowing the score . . . something like that.
All you can do is sing wildly and hope it'll finish
So joyous and refreshing that you gape with awe.

When Stuff Is Tough

One thing I hardly ever manage the grace to say
To my children when they are struggling is how
Proud I am about them when they are struggling.
I just can't find easy ways to slip it into the fray,
But I feel it enormously. Sounds condescending
And trite and boringly paternal when I articulate
It, though, or try to. Sounds like a smug old guy
Lecturing the muddled young, and what a cliché
That is, you know? But I feel it so deeply I can't
Stop thinking about it: thus this miniscule poem.
A lot of the ways you love is when stuff is tough.
There's not even a way to say that easily and we
All know what I mean. A lot of love is attending
To how people you love stand up again defiantly
After being rattled and rocked. A lot of daditude
Is watching, and wincing, and feeling something
Like joyous rage that they refuse to quit. Lots of
Being a dad, it turns out, is being reminded what
To remember. I always thought it would be great
If I could take all their pain on me, but that turns
Out to be exactly wrong—they have to thrash on
Their own, and I have to watch, pained and awed.

A Million Prayers

The first time we visited my sister in her monastery
Was just after one of our sons had survived massive
Surgeries, before and during which all the monks &
Nuns in the monastery, not to mention thousands of
Other generous souls, had prayed constantly for him;
And it turned out that they had gone over the million
Prayer mark for our son, which, according to the law
Of the monastery, gave him lifetime privileges. He's
No dolt, this kid, and he took off running, to hammer
On drums, and eat the cookies on an altar, and pursue
The grim local peacocks, who were deeply aggrieved.
By the time we retrieved him he was worn and happy
And the peacocks were huddled bitterly in the maples.
Even now I sometimes wonder if he will end up there
In his golden years, maybe retiring there at age ninety
And serving as the soul who calls everyone to prayer;
He did exactly that when he was a small boy, after all.

Poem in Which My Mom Goes to Get the Mail

Which is not at all as direct and straightforward as it sounds,
Mom being past 90 and wielding her walker like a shillelagh.
Starting in the bedroom, she cuts past the couch, up the step
Into the kitchen, past her older husband (a bit of chaff there),
Down two steps into the yard, and then under the basketball
Hoop toward the mailbox in the street—all told Odyssea has
Traveled forty yards, let's say, and an idiot with a timepiece
Would note that it took her about fifteen minutes and serious
Effort. But the idiot, like her husband at the table, savors her
Grace and guts in the matter of the mail. She loads it all into
The cloth bag attached to her walker and turns toward home,
Not unlike a beautiful ship heading to harbor. There are more
Moments of silent grace and courage than we could calculate
In two lifetimes. It used to make me sad that I would miss so
Much, but now I'm delighted to see what is right there to see.
Even better is the knowledge that *you* know just what I mean.

A Lot of Not

Say you have three kids. Or *had* three kids—now
They're grown and mostly out. They stop by here
And there, & camp out when they are flummoxed,
But mostly there is a lot of not where they used to
Be shouting and leaving those damned wet towels
On the floor and barking at each other and snoring
Late into the afternoon and deftly avoiding chores.
All the places they used to be are insistently empty.
This is unnerving, to say the least. I still sometimes
Make them sandwiches without thinking. You slap
Together a second sandwich while humming music
And then you just stand still, feeling weird. No one
Is more delighted that they are launched, but here's
A sandwich without a kid to snarf it in six seconds.
I give it to the dog, and he gobbles it, but he knows
Full well why he got it, and each of us knows what
The other one is thinking, and we go watch jays for
A while, probably because their raucous rude verve
Reminds us of what we both love, and miss terribly.

Buried in a military cemetery in a deep forest
About an hour away. There's oak and cypress
And pine. This will happen, I guess, and then
He'll be a thin kid again somehow or the most
Deft of the falcon chicks or the willow branch
That finally figures out how to sip from a lake
All easy and casual, like it didn't take practice.

Do You Remember Being Born?

Do you remember being born? I ask a boy, age five.
No, he says, but my *mom* says she will never forget
That day. She says I came out smiling and laughing
About something. She says that she asked me what
Was so funny and I said it was a joke someone told
Just before I came through her door. She says I *will*
Remember the joke someday, and maybe even who
Told it, and when that happens she wants me to call
Her *right away*. She says I have not stopped smiling
Since I was born but *that's* not true—look, I am not
Smiling right now! But he couldn't hold his unsmile
More than an instant, and both of us started laughing.

Clairtonica Street

Our dad never spoke about his childhood at all when
We were kids. We would ask him and he would chat
About this and that and the other thing; we were easy
To distract, and dad was gentle and funny and to hear
Him on any subject was a pleasure. Many years went
By, and then the sons decided to haul him back to his
Native Pittsburgh. We were checking genealogy. But
When we drove up a snowy hill, and found the house
He had lived in as a child, he burst into tears. We had
Never seen dad cry before, none of us. We sat quietly.
My brothers and our father are big tall guys and there
Was a sort of long big tall quiet in the van. Very large
Men being silent is a *sound*. Good thing no one spoke.
Any words right then would have been a sort of insult.
We could talk about after, and how our father opened
The gates and told us everything, all the pain and loss,
All the ways he created his gentle quiet wry manhood,
All the wit and dignity and love and patience and guts,
All the ways his life was a song of grace and gratitude,
But let's all just sit here in the back seat of the old van.
Give the man time with his tears. He waited something
Like seventy years to cry those tears. You have to give
Those tears some space and some respect. In a moment
He'll say, gentle as always, *that's my house! my house!*,
But now let's just sit and revere him from the back seat.

Bar Brawl

Yes, I was in one. In Chicago, many years ago.
A blues bar, not noticeably rough, on a Sunday;
You would think the odds would be against fist
In eye and smash of glass and table overturning
And guys picking up pool cues. The bartenders
Punched guys. I saw a woman throwing drinks.
Yes, it was terrifying. This was not some movie
Gig where it's choreographed. This was savage
And sudden and there is screaming. I see a man
Swing a pool cue like a bat and hit another man
With the sound of a pumpkin smashing. It ends
In about two minutes with one guy unconscious.
I never did find out why it started—I was afraid
To ask, and afraid to leave too soon, too, in case
I'd get blamed. I was *afraid*, is what I am trying
To say. I'm not trying to draw some conclusions
Here—I just want to record a moment we've all
Endured, and we do not talk about. We ought to,
You know. There's no shame in it. We all drank
From the terror cup. I have friends who got shot
At and they were terrified, and I know men who
Were lost in forests, and we've all been terrified
In traffic accidents. This has nothing whatsoever
To do with courage or heroism. It's about saying
Honestly *man, I was so scared I couldn't breathe.*
Maybe if we say it honestly, then somehow we'll
Find a way to at least cut back on times when it's

Our fault. Maybe we could outthink our own old
Urge to make *other* people scared. It worked for
Us for a million years, but now it doesn't so well,
You know? I'll stop—but you think this one over.

Poem in Which Two Brothers, Ages Four and Six, Examine Their Newest Brother, Aged Three Days

I was not around when my older sister and brothers were born,
And when my next-youngest brother was born I was just a year
Old myself, but when our last brother was born we were awake
And riveted by what he would be like. *What* a disappointment!
For one thing you could hardly see him in his ocean of blankets.
First chance we got we peeled him and spread him out on a bed.
He was no bigger than a sneaker and was just about as energetic.
No matter where you poked him he didn't do anything, even cry.
Ironically this infant would grow up to be about six foot twenty
And strong enough to beat up all brothers at once, but back then
He was a lump the size of a squirrel. You could almost see how
Someday he might have hairs. He just lay there looking up at us
Expectantly. You wouldn't believe people arrived in such small
Doses, but then again you couldn't believe this peaceful squirrel
Had lived inside mom. She'd been huge, and *this* was the result?
We felt almost a little cheated—like she should have had eleven
Of these things. *Then* we could have some fun—we'd command
An army! Little did we know that this shoe would be the coolest
Brother ever, the kind you would pick out of a brother catalogue
If you took your time and carefully checked the parts that matter.
After a few minutes somebody old came in to rescue the squirrel
And yell at us for peeling it down to the nuts. We didn't confess
That it had peed like a racehorse on the sheet—it wasn't *our* bed.

The Miracle Is That We All Believe There Is a Miracle

If you were never an altar boy, you never knew
What it was like to sit motionless in the sacristy
And savor dust motes and the sunlight fingering
Its way through the mullioned windows and the
Gravelly shamble of Father's boots on the walk;
If you listened hard you could hear him hesitate
By the statue of Mary; he would touch her hand
Sometimes, if he needed private assistance. You
Would be polishing the paten as he wandered in,
And he would make a sort of bearish sound, and
Robe up, and if there had been enough coffee he
Would say something witty about the poor Mets.
It was a performance, you see, and we were two
Teammates, and each knew what the other could
Do, strong points and weak points, and an awful
Lot was said without anything being said. That's
What I think about most now when I think about
Those shimmering mornings. The quiet language
Of linen and wine and wafers and our poor Mets.
There was a pew by the door to the altar, and I'd
Sit there and wait. I went first, carrying the cross,
Followed by Father with The Book held high; he
Waved it above his head like a wild miracle to be
Marveled over. He knew his theater, o yes he did.
Sometimes we would outnumber the congregants,
But he played to a full house every time, not once

Even trimming his sermon. We had to admire him
For that. It's table talk with stories, and a mystery
Guest arriving without ado, he'd say. People think
The miracle is the elevation of the host but it's not.
The miracle is that we all believe there's a miracle.
If we didn't believe in the unbelievable there is no
Mass and no Church either, and then where would
We be? The Church is a vocabulary for that for which
We have weak words. Are you getting *any* of this?

Poem for Dorothy Stafford

I knew a lady who had no right arm, *right from the start*,
As she said, smiling gently. She was so deft with the left
That you didn't even notice, the first few times you were
With her. You just assumed her right arm was bruised or
Something and being held close to home. The more time
You spent with her, the more you liked her. She was that
Kind of person. She knew who she was, but she was very
Much interested in who you were. She liked to listen. I'll
Always remember that. She died yesterday. One morning
I sat with her at a lunch and we began to speculate where
Her right arm was. Nebraska maybe, where she was born,
Or loaned somehow, to someone on another planet. "Can
It be living on its own?' she said. 'That would be a poem.'

Poem for My Uncle
on His Hundredth Birthday

Let's pick one moment, from any number of candidates.
The year is 1929. Let's say it's December, and snowing;
This *is* Pittsburgh, you know. My uncle is sixteen years
Old and he has been saving money to go to Notre Dame
Since he was eight years old. He has done every kind of
Job a kid can do those years: he has shoveled and carted
And carried and dug and planted and delivered and built
And repaired and painted and invested, and he's got just
Enough for freshman year—that's six hundred and fifty
Dollars, which will pay for tuition, room, food, laundry,
But not books. He's not worried about the books. Those
He can borrow. His dad calls him into the warm kitchen.
They sit at the table. The news is delivered. Grandfather
Rests his hand on his oldest son's shoulder for a moment
And then goes down into the city to look for work. Right
Here, now, here's the moment for us to watch. My uncle
Sits silently at the kitchen table. There's a radio burbling
Somewhere, and his brother and mother upstairs. Where
They live, away up on a hill, on the west side of the city,
You can see hawks a lot. It's snowing but not really hard.
He just sits there, staring at the snow. In a while he'll get
Up, and proceed, and go into insurance, and marry twice,
And have seven children, and be famous among nephews
For being the quietest smilingest calmest uncle in history,

But let's just sit with him at this kitchen table for a while.
His whole life just broke and the snow didn't even pause
But we can. Let's watch reverently as he gathers himself
And starts over. The snow will finish just before nightfall.

The Raccoon Kit

One time I watched raccoon kits being born.
Did I ever tell you that story? No? This was
Years ago. The mother raccoon had denned
In an ancient elm. The tree had aged in such
A way that I could just see into the bole she
Had chosen, if I crept out on a roof and laid
One eye over a tiny crack; yes, I was scared
She would notice a vast eye and puncture it,
But she didn't. The kits emerged wetly, and
Slowly, and there were three of them—then
A fourth, but this one never moved. I'm old
Now, and that was fifty years ago a raccoon
Child was born without a breath. But I have
Never forgotten the instant that I realized it,
And was briefly breathless myself, with loss
And sorrow and amazement. I crawled back
Along the roof of the garage. It's easy to say
There is a profligacy of life, and so of death,
But still I wonder if that life went elsewhere;
And I would bet a buck you wonder this too.

Silentium

We think and talk and tell only the most dramatic
Times; when the boy was carried off for surgeries
And there was every chance his grin would never
Come back; the broken shoulder and the weeping
In a corner with his hood down over his face until
His father came to save him; but here he is gazing
At his report card and his hands cover his face. To
Watch him from the corner of my eye and not talk
Is awfully hard but that is what has to happen. We
Will talk later, maybe. We hardly ever admit stuff
About love that doesn't sound good; nothing hurts
As much as love does, and that's a fact. The water
Boils and I drop the noodles in; that's all I can say.

Hoop

I was sprawled on a deck in the sun recently when a child
Said how come you don't have any hair on your ankles if
There's all that hair on your legs and feet and even toes??
And I explained that I used to be a total fanatic basketball
Player who played two to four hours a day from age eight
Until I was Christ's age, and then my back busted, so that
Was that, but I had taped my ankles so tightly so carefully
So methodically with such meticulous obsessive attention
For so many years that long ago the hair had been yanked
Out when I peeled off the tapes after games and practices;
And while the girl, either bored or more probably thinking
I was a raving loony, wandered off to commit small crime,
I sat there on the deck in the sun remembering many many
Hundreds of hours taping my ankles just right so that they
Wouldn't buckle and lurch and splay so that I could sprint
And leap and spin with a touch more abandon, just a little;
And for the first time in my life I was happy I would never
Have hair on my ankles again, for that meant I could never
Forget the game that gave me thousands of joyous minutes.
By my count I spent four years of my life inside basketball,
And the sweet Lord alone knows I would have tripled that,
If I could. Not in this life, any more; but maybe the next. . . .

Wrenness

What if you sat down to write a poem,
But the poem forgot what it was it was
Supposed to be about, and both of you
Had to thrash around there in the room
For a while looking under the cushions
And flipping open books on the theory
That maybe you were using the idea as
A bookmark, until the poem says Hey!
I remember, it was wrens! They skitter,
Remember we were going to poke into
That? And you say yes!, their liquidity!
So the poem closes here with wrens on
Your mind, with *wrenness*; what if, eh?

At a High School This Morning

I was visiting a High School this morning
And babbling on about stories being wild
Holy nutritious necessary amazing crucial
Meals, and a girl raises her hand, and I say
Yes ma'am? And she whispers what if you
Can't write because everything is smashed
And you want to write so bad but you can't
Because everything is broken? what should
I do then? what should I *do?* And there was
This silence that was so tender I have to tell
You about it. No one looked away. Nothing
Was said, either, which I thought was grace.
After a minute I tried to be reverent and say
Something substantive and attentive but it's
All a muddle, what helps and doesn't. After
Class the teacher told me yup, for that child
Everything is smashed, no details necessary,
But she has never missed an assignment yet
And she turns in work early, and she has the
Most astounding imaginative leaps you ever
Saw. Grading her stuff is the purest pleasure.
You never saw a kid happier to be told what
To try with her imagination, due by Monday.
She must huddle in her assignments all night
Sometimes, stretching them out so they will

Last until morning. There's a lot of kids like
Her, sad to say. Maybe stories are like small
Safe houses for kids like that. We should all
Remember that, when we chat about stories.

Cutting

My two younger brothers and I are sitting at the dining room table.
We are cutting up brown paper bags to use as covers for textbooks.
We are eight and ten and twelve years old. School started Monday.
Mom gave us three large bags each because she knows we will cut
Poorly until we get the hang of the thing. She was going to help us,
But she had to leave, and grandma will help. She sits reluctantly at
The table, close to the youngest. She likes him and does not like us.
He is small and gentle and the kindest kid ever and we are not. She
Cuts the rectangles deftly for his spelling and math books and then
Folds the paper with beautifully sharp edges and tapes them tightly
Over the covers of his books so the covers are taut russet meadows
Ripe for his name and the teacher's name which she writes for him.
My next brother down waits patiently for grandma to help him. His
Face is so open and loving and expectant. You never met a sweeter
Kid in your life. I don't have the heart to tell him that grandma will
Not help him. She will not help me, either. I am a wild rude ruffian
Who will not end well. Because my next brother runs with me he is
Also a ruffian although he is not a ruffian at all. He puts his scissors
Near the brown paper bags so grandma can reach them easily. Even
At age twelve, even at the lip of my vulgar teenage years, even then
Sometimes I could see pain coming for someone else and felt awful
About it. She doesn't even look at us. She will never reach for those
Scissors. I know this and he doesn't and I feel awful. Finally I reach
For his scissors and start cutting his paper and grandma says I ought
To keep my hands to myself and even then, even when I was a child,
I remember thinking how could you love someone and not like them
At all, how was that possible? Probably I got in trouble but not much.

Probably grandma said something but mom knew how to read under
The words. Probably grandma was a real generous person sometimes.
Probably I actually was a ruffian. But there is my brother, waiting so
Patiently. I couldn't stand it. Maybe it's good to do a bad thing, once
In a while. Maybe bad things are good sometimes. Maybe it depends
On all sorts of stuff, and good and bad are some weird kind of lovers
Who don't like each other but need each other desperately. Could be.

Song to Hum While Opening Mail from a Friend

O the very fact that there are friends who write with their hands
Even if just the forefingers hammering away on keyboards, and
Also then print out the resulting muddle and scrawl and scribble
And pop it in the post-box! The lickable areas on the envelopes!
The Return Address Just in Case! The choice of stamps, and we
All blessedly have friends who carefully choose their stamps, &
Stand in line at the post-office asking for the ones with Authors,
Or members of the Simpson family, or stamps with Polar Bears!
And the fact that there are fifty addresses in your memory, some
Of them no longer inhabited by the people you loved to write to;
Much like your mind retains past phone numbers and exchanges,
Like Mayfair and Ludlow and Allegheny and Cypress and Tulip!
And the fact that you can draw all morning on an envelope or by
God paint it flagrantly with horses and angels, and your postman
Will deliver it anyway! Probably grinning at the nut who mailed
It to you! And you can put a few grains of sand inside your note,
From the beach we went to as children, or a feather from a hawk
Who glared in the window like an insurance adjuster with talons,
Or a painting by a child, or a photograph of four of the names of
That which we call God for lack of a better label. Even the folds
Of the paper, and the paperness of the paper, and the fact that it's
All about miracles and affection, which is to say, of course, love!
Sure it is. All the good parts are about love, in all its many masks.

The Blue Room

I was in a library in Utah the other night when
A small boy asked me to help him find a book.
The boy was perhaps four years old and intent.
I said what book would you like, little brother?
And he said 'One with blue in it. A *lot* of blues.
One I can smell the blue. I *love* that blue. Mom
Says people can like other colors too, but why?
Is there a shelf for blue books? If lots of people
Read the book does the blue wear out? Is there
A blue bank where you have to get a new blue?'
You know, many times I have sighed that I am
Not able to help people who ask me for advice,
Or directions, or counsel about this or that. But
I don't think I ever wanted so much to say, hey,
Little brother, come with me to the room where
All the books are so blue that you have to laugh
At the seethe and soar of it; books about oceans
And herons and jays and the sky and Vida Blue,
Books about how blue used to be and might yet
Become, books brimming with azure and cobalt
And cornflower and iris and periwinkle and teal,
Books so blue that you dream in blue for days. . . .

One Night in Powell's Bookstore in Oregon

You want to know what writing is capable of, why it matters?
Listen, last night I did a brief reading in a bookstore, and then
Signed books and chatted with folks, always a sweet and odd
Experience, because they don't really care about me defacing
Their books with my headlong scrawled signature as much as
They want to *say* something, and not even really to me. There
Is something that needs to be articulated, sometimes haltingly,
About how my story hit their story, about how my tale is *their*
Tale, you know what I mean? I have learned to shut my mouth
And wait and listen. And last night when she came to the head
Of the line a woman held out my book and burst into tears and
Then laughed so shy and happy and embarrassed and surprised
By herself that she started to cry again. I sort of knew what she
Meant and said thank you and she laughed again and a tall boy
Behind her held out his book. That's what writing is for, seems
To me. To try to lay words on wordless things we all know but
Find hard to say. I think it's silly to scribble my scrawl in what
Turns out to be their story, but I do it with reverence. So much
Of what matters we have not the faintest idea why but o it does,
It does and does and does: I cannot find a word for how it does.

On Witing a Poem Without the R on You Keyboad

See, I can't even get past the title of the thing without . . . that lette.
People make such a fuss about E being the essential keystoke but
Me pesonally I am going to go with the one that elevates so many
Of my sentences. Just a brief sampling would include remarkable,
Reverence, irrepressible, redolence, roaring, rapacious, rapturous,
And raptor—none of which would have heft or veve or a glint of
Claity without their aahs, as you would say in Boston. You smile
At this and so do I but maybe things like this happen in some odd
Way to make us stop and see, just fo a flash, the huge of the tiny?

Kirkwood

There was a street in my town called Kirkwood that really did
Have kirks and woods—four churches in a mile, and two little
Gangs of dense trees that somehow had eluded the hungry axe.
There was a Jewish temple, a Catholic church, a Lutheran kirk,
And a church of Saint Thomas Christians, who were relatively
Catholic, as my dad explained; they were basically our remote
Cousins, like the Lutherans, whereas the temple was more like
Our grandfather; remember that Christ was Jewish, and a rabbi
To boot, as my dad said. We were happily confused. Our mom
Thought that perhaps Kirkwood Avenue was zoned for religion
To keep the faiths in concourse if not as yet in amiable concert,
As she said: Also you have to count the copses as churches too,
Not only historically, as reflective of ancient spiritual practices,
But in every sense the direct and immutable evidence of a God,
Which is to say the Creative Energy that through the green fuse
Drives the flower, that whirls the water in the pool, that sets the
Stars to spin in their appointed rounds. Yes, we sat there gaping
In the kitchen as our dad strode over to her and said This is why
I love you, and they kissed, and we were horrified, and gagging;
But under our wailing as their kiss persisted was something like
A faint understanding that he was saying thanks for the way she
Was miraculously who she was, and that kissing can be praying.

Poem About My Late Brother Kevin's Body

Boy, it was a whopper of a body, is the first thing to say.
A capacious being for a capacious soul. Huge mustache;
Walrussian, is the best explanation. The word withering
Was invented for his glare. He was a tall skinny praying
Mantis as a teenager but then he was essentially bearish,
Or *ursine*, as he would say quietly. With a hint of a grin.
He had ratty knees. Oh, I get the whole cremation thing,
But today I refuse to acknowledge ashes in a buried box.
I refuse. I disacknowledge. I insist that what is so is not.
Today he is backing down the lane slow as snow while I
Decide to pick one coast or the other of his epic rear end
And dash out and steal the ball because it's damn certain
I can't shoulder him and keep him from inching glacially
To the basket with that incredibly frustrating metronomic
Dribble, steady as a heartbeat, until he is about six inches
From the basket and throws up that silly stupid tiny hook
That never misses. You can't tell me he's not hitting that
Maddening little ballerina hook shot; not today you can't.
That shot wins the game too and our next brother steps in
Because he has winners and Kevin admits a hint of a grin
And I am staying here all afternoon until I beat him again.
You guys can go to the cemetery if you like but I got next.

Poem for a Friend's Dying Dad

I only met the man the once, and he seemed like an affable enough
Guy, cheerful and avuncular, but what do we know of anyone then,
Amid the rattle of cocktails and the burble of small talk and the hey
Where did we hang our jackets we really better get going? And yes,
I listened to all the sad awful stories about the man and his troubles,
Some of which will scar generations to come. But he is my friend's
Dad, and you only get the one dad, with total respect for stepfathers
And gentle responsible uncles and even husbands who serve as their
Wives' missing dads in mysterious ways. He's her *dad,* and there he
Is, fading away by the piano. He cradled her when she was little and
Helped her with her Halloween costume and sat with her at the table
Thrashing through geometry homework. He didn't work out the way
She wanted him to, needed him to, and it's easy to castigate the man;
But I guess I just see him at the kitchen table, with the history report
That she has to finish tomorrow. He's reading her paper for mistakes
While she gets just the right color for the cover and he finds the clips
That will look coolest holding it all together. There's no arguing that
He did not hold it all together very well, that's for sure, for whatever
Reasons, none of them my business. But just for a moment, though I
Hardly knew the man, I feel some weird pang for him. He must have
Kicked himself a million times for not being at the tiny kitchen table
More, or better, or enough. I feel awful for my friend, who will have
An even bigger hole in her heart now than the gaping chasm she had;
But for a minute here as the sun goes down I think of her poor father.
All you ever really want as a father is not to be a bad one, in the end.
That's all you can aim for. Maybe somehow he'll get another chance.

The Window Through Which to Whisper

Talked to six high-school students this morning,
Two young men and four young women, for 20
Minutes each. Ostensibly the discussion was all
About college admission essays, but one thing I
Have learned in life is to be quiet and listen and
Out will pour real honest naked hard holy grace,
And there it was, child after lanky child. So very
Many masks worn as armor. So many polite bits
Of college admission essays that skated over the
Stories they were so desperate to tell they would
Even tell *me*—given the chance, the shy window
Through which to whisper. When we were done
I stood up rattled and blessed. Such terrible gifts
And such generosity in the giving. I remembered
Confession, in the old days, when the old shutter
Made of oak or pine would shiver open suddenly
And a voice, often so calm and gentle, would say
Say what it is you most want to say, and have not.

Reverencing His Bones

My father is sitting in his chair by his desk telling me a story
About the leggy girl with the cascade of black hair and o my
God those perfect teeth in the photo from the war when they
Were just married and as he rumbles I am running my hands
Over the bones of his shoulders. He doesn't have any muscle
There any more, it seems. It's all bone. He has been whittled
By his century, and he was a big guy too. He is still tall—but
Curved tall, as one of his grandsons says. That is my favorite
Photograph of your mom ever, he says. I feel where his bicep
Used to adamantly be. Boy, that room was so tiny I could not
Stand up straight except in the middle. I keep reverencing his
Bones; his shoulder blades could slice his shirt. Seventy years
Ago *that* was, he says. I weighed then probably what I weigh
Now, with expansion in the middle, like our pot-bellied planet.
I have hardly ever felt his shoulders, I realize. Certainly when
I was little and he carried me but then not again for fifty years
Until now; and for a few more minutes it stays gloriously now.

One Reason We Invented the Poem
Is to Try to Say What Cannot Be Said

For many years I worked for a man who drove me stark raving mad.
He was the worst meticulous fussy fidgety perfectionist control freak
In the history of human beings. He would rather that things were way
Late than that they were done with any hint of a mistake. We did not
See eye to eye about this, or much else. Yet no one cared more about
The work we did, and what it meant. He was subject to fits of temper,
And you never met a gentler man. He held grudges, and was the soul
Of mercy beyond sense and reason. He was a pacifist who had earned
A Bronze Star in a war. He was the worst manager I ever saw and the
Best employee. He had been a quiet drunk and when he realized he'd
Damage his new children he stopped and never took another sip. Lots
Of people knew him and no one knew him well. He wouldn't allow it.
Yet he wept easily when he was shivered, which he was every blessed
Day, usually by something having to do with a child. He was so close
With his emotions that you wanted to scream but no one was courtlier.
He took his faith so seriously that no one was ever more furious about
Its crimes and lies and greed for money and power. He retired at dawn
This morning. He cleaned out his office and went home and sent email
To a few people. Even his leaving was meticulously controlled so that
No one could say farewell or tell him they admired him; I have to grin
At the sheer consistency of that. But one reason we invented the poem
Is to try to say what cannot be said, and what I want to say is that I am
So thankful for your honesty, your integrity, your patient commitment
To work that in the end was about the holiness of tall children. I won't
Forget that, as long as I live. It would have been cool to tell you that in
Person but you won't allow that, you brilliant oddity, so here's a poem.

Poem for a New Baby Girl

Listen, this is the best world *ever*. You should know that
Right off the bat. No matter what happens, that's the fact.
Now, a lot of things will happen, and they will not all be
Peaches and excellent cigars, my small friend. People do
Go and die on you. And cops give you tickets for taillight
Infractions and your dad, no matter what he says, could *not*
Shoot a basketball at all with his left hand. But remember
The first line of this poem, my friend. There's never been
A world like this, swirling with love and laughter and tall
Cousins and your cool mom and the beach and pears, and
The wonderful gift of brilliant and handsome great-uncles.
Some poems might end right there, but this one has to say:
Welcome. You are loved way more than you know. That's
Proof of the first line of this poem—never ever forget that.

The Luckier Man

in memory of the late great Dick Hayward

I knew a man once who taught me a sweet lesson without a word:
He sent me a wedding present. It was an umbrella. This is Oregon,
So it was a particularly apt and suitable and thoughtful gift. Here's
The thing, though: he was the father of my lovely bride's longtime
Boyfriend, the guy she almost married but didn't. So let us review:
A man sent me a deft wedding gift even though I was the man who
Was marrying the girl his son had loved for years, and sure the dad
Loved her too, she's that kind of woman, the dad was sad when the
Young couple broke up. But he was delighted that she was married
To someone she loved, he told me years later, and of course he sent
Me a present, out of affection for her and respect for me, the luckier
Man. So it was that yet again I learned about grace, and about being
An actual man, not just being the size of a man, or dressing like one.

Poem for the Older Woman
Who Tripped & Fell Headlong
Suddenly by the Woodpile

The fact is that we met the once, and had about four minutes total
Of interested conversation, largely about leaping dogs and shower
Engineering, but all the rest of my life I will remember the minute
When gravity hauled you down by the woodpile. Your dog leaped
Anxiously; I stood there helplessly, as I can no longer bend down;
But to my amazement you were as calm as the sea just after dawn.
I suppose that's what this poem is about. I thought that was pretty
Cool, to stay so calm when the evidence was all for fear and worry.
That was a lesson to me. Yes, you wriggled your way to being tall
Again, and we got back to the matters at hand, but your eerie calm
Stays with me. I don't know the shape of your life, and the history
Of your love and pains, but there was an amused grace that minute
That was maybe revelatory of something; say *character* or *courage*
If you have to use words, I guess. But there are way more eloquent
Things than words, and that moment by Hidden Cove is one for me.

Poem for the Reverend Bill Harper Just Before People Come After His Private Parts with Sharp Weaponry

Aw, I could razz you about the whole Reverend
Thing, but I know you well enough to know you
Think it's funny too, inasmuch as everything we
Can see and not see is reverence. I am not saying
I know you well, though; I mean, we would have
To be brothers or guys who meet every ninth day
For a pint to even begin to think we dug some of
The other guy's deep tides; but we *get* each other,
I think. You know what I mean. The humor, wine,
Pain, wild holy kids, being delighted and puzzled
By marriage and the finer points of pension plans;
Hawks, friends, decent pens, people leaning on us
As they weep. We share that language, am I right?
So here's what I say to you, brother. You couldn't
Even begin to count the beings who love you. Hey,
I am only a guy doing his best and often stumbling,
Just like you, and I am sure not wise—but if a man
Cannot begin to count the oceans of love slathered
In his personal direction, then he is rich far beyond
Calculation. Remember to be rich when fear comes.
The only thing to do with fear is to tell it to piss off
And laugh with all your might as you say it, brother.
We will be laughing too and there's no more honest
Prayer than that. Or, here, let me quote my brothers;
If a lot of people love you, you are not the idiot you
Think you are. Keep that in mind now. *We* sure will.

The Rough Prince

One hot night many years ago when I was a boy
My oldest brother, then tall and thin and taciturn,
Donned buckskins and leggings and face paints
And danced wildly and amazingly with similarly
Adorned lanky boys at public event for Scouting.
I disremember the details, if it was a fundraising
Event or the epic closing of some sort of festival,
But I remember sitting there awed and frightened
In a huddle in the dark with my younger brothers.
We had never seen our oldest brother without his
Somber terse cold grim prickly testy flinty dignity:
We had never seen him *abandoned*. I'm sure now
That he was shy and sweet and gentle, and just as
Scared as we all are all our lives of not being who
We want to be or who we want others to see us as,
But we didn't see that then; we saw only the rough
Prince who was going to leave the family, as quick
As he could, through doors marked navy or college,
The one who fought dad, the one who spoke coldly
To mom, the one whose scornful glare could easily
Whip us upstairs to cry. We so wanted him to love
Us and we didn't think he did and later we realized
He did but only through chinks in his armor; it was
A prison for him too, his awful dignity; and so we
Sat in the dark at the powwow, thrilled and amazed
At the howling whirling brother we had never met.
I suppose later he came home and washed off paint,

And folded and boxed up his dancing uniform, and
Strapped on his stern again, but let's not get to that.
Let's back up to where he has just leapt into the air
So high that for a second you think he'll never land.

A Whopping Poem

Need not be *gargantuan*, though, know what I mean?
It could be epic while remaining lean; terse and huge
At once, if we find the right subject. A child's defiant
Grace under duress, her adamant laughter, his tireless
Courage without the slightest reason to be brave. She
Has a bone marrow transplant today. He is once again
All too familiar with the murmur of the infusion room.
We don't talk about this much because it's just too big.
We just can't handle kids suffering—they're too small,
I think. You want to hear something huge, though? Go
Listen to a nurse or a teacher in the humming corridors
Of the floors with the most pain. They'll tell you some
Whopping stories and they only use a few small words.

Haiku Haiku

How come no one ever
Admits how hard it is
To count all these syllables?
Or admits that we use
Our fingers to do so
While cursing Basho?

The Prison of Shyness

Pop, asks son two, did you ever have a crush on a girl and do nothing
About it? And there I am in high school, watching her board the 5:20
Bus, the last one after all the sports were finished with practices. Did
I ever once even say hello or wave or make a stupid joke or ask about
Homework or remark on weather or comment on the war in Vietnam
Or ask about her family or in any way whatsoever indicate to her that
I would like to establish a bridgehead so as to somehow cross her sea?
I did not. But there I was every blessed day. There are so many funny
Things to say, of course, about my idiocies, and the prison of shyness,
About how perhaps the poor girl actually did like me, and might have
Said so given the slightest opening, about what a dolt I was to huddle
In the doorway of the gym, rain or shine, about how sometimes I took
The fastest shower in the history of ever so as to be there five minutes
Early because sometimes the bus driver left a minute or four early just
To aggravate me, about how even the time she missed the bus and had
To stand there for thirteen minutes alone waiting for her mom to arrive
To drive her home I did not emerge from the shadows of the gym door
But stood there like the worst speechless terrified idiot who ever lived;
Well, there are gobs of Entertaining Observations to be made. But let's
Not make them. Instead let's admit that you stood there too, and today,
Right about now, there are a million kids in a million doorways staring
At a million other kids they would love to say hi to. It takes us forever
To get out of the prison of ourselves, doesn't it? And we never do step
All the way out of the doorway, I suppose. But just for a moment, here
At the end, remember how it felt, and maybe we can shove one kid out
Of his doorway, and he says, quietly, *hello*, and she, no kidding, smiles.

Poem for a Son Going Off to College

Looking at photographs of the kids. One of them is going
To college tomorrow. I used to wear that kid like a jacket.
He fell asleep instantly given the slightest chance. School,
The car, even once during a time-out at a basketball game,
Although to be fair he was the point guard and had played
The whole first half and been double-teamed. He could be
Laughing at something and you turned away to see a hawk
Or his lissome mom and when you turned back he was out.
But tomorrow he's in the top bunk in a room far away. We
Will leave the back porch light on for him out of habit and
In the morning we will both notice that it's still on and one
Of us will cry right into the coffee beans and the other will
Remember that it felt like all the poems we mean when we
Say words like *dad* and *son* and *love* when I slung that boy
Over one shoulder or another or carried him amidships like
A sack of rice or best of all dangling him by his feet so that
All the nickels he put in his pockets for just this eventuality
Poured down like something else we do not have words for.

October Poem

What is the best poem you ever wrote in your whole life?
I ask a friend of mine, aged six, and she thinks about this
For a whole minute, looking down in the grass for words,
And she says, The time I tried to make a coat for a mouse
From spider-webs. My sister and brothers helped me find
The webs. It takes a *lot* of webs to make a jacket for mice.
We apologized to the spiders. This was in October. Mama
Said we could borrow webs as long as we were respectful.
That's the best poem I ever wrote, and I didn't do it alone.

Fluid Mechanics

Sitting in a chapel high in the golden sculpted hills of California
A few minutes before Mass I reach down to a small wooden box
By my chair, where missals and songbooks are stored, and I find
A set of ancient eyeglasses folded into an old cloth case, so worn
That it feels like a pelt, and I realize that my chair must belong to
A certain sister here at the old mission. Maybe she's here at Mass,
Trying not to be annoyed that I snagged her seat. After Mass I ask
Around and a sweet sister with a cane says o no, dear, that's Sister
Maureen Mary's seat. She passed over two years ago. She was tall
And hilarious and subject to fits of darkness. She'd been a student
Of engineering, a really brilliant girl, when she decided to join our
Community. Her parents were appalled, or as Sister Maureen liked
To say, aghast. She became a wonderful teacher with us. When she
Died we got hundreds of letters from her former students. Teachers
Have to cultivate the long view, as Sister said herself. You haven't
Much immediate evidence of your labors. But you get flashes, here
And there, and hugs at the end of the year, she would say. She was
Still an engineer, she said, still actually working in fluid mechanics.
Her mom and dad began to visit us once a year and then more often.
Her sister never visited even once although she sent money. Sister's
Parents died and willed us the truck in which they came to visit their
Daughter. We use it all over the place. You'll see it go by today, for
Certain. When Sister died we left her glasses there just for moments
Like this, when someone discovers her. Often it is us, of course, and
We laugh, but then you spend the rest of the day remembering Sister
Maureen Mary, who is a most remarkable soul, whom I miss terribly.

The Lakes of Ohio

Indeed I did deliver mine own child, says the slight smiling man.
We were deep in the woods, and our child decided his hour was
Come and so it did. His mother was startled. We'd gone to swim.
She loved the water because it carried their dual weight patiently.
She was in the center of the lake and she cried out and said God!
And right then our son began to change worlds. We did not have
Time to get all the way to shore but she swam hard and I dove to
Catch the baby should he or she slip away from us. Yes, terrified,
Sure. But by grace he was not born until we were in the shallows.
He made a soft splash as I caught him. His mother, she did kneel
And weep. On the shore we made a bed of moss and fern and she
Lay with him and I cut the cord between them. Though their cord
Has never been broken since. That is a grace also. There are more
Graces than we know or could measure did we have the machines
Of genius. We all go back to that lake quite often. Very nearly we
Named the boy for the lake, but it's called mud, and that wouldn't
Be a right name. You cannot name a boy Mud in good conscience.
However we did then examine the lakes of Ohio for his right name,
And that is how our son Isaac came to be called so. Our next child
Was a boy also and he is called Abram, and our daughter is Aurora,
Names that are also the names of lakes in Ohio. We visit each lake,
Trying to take turns to be fair. But it seems to me we do visit Isaac
More than we do the others. I hate to admit it, but I believe it is so.
Do Abram and Aurora complain about this? Only every other day!

Te Absolvo

Of course we remember everything that ever happened to us.
Sure we do. We can easily make a concerted effort to forget,
And successfully forget from Levels One through Eight, but
You remember, somehow—at the cellular or molecular level
Perhaps, where shame and embarrassment are in cold storage.
The things you most want to forget are the things you cannot.
You can *say*, as I have, that you have no memory of that evil
Minute when you lied or cheated or dodged responsibility or
Worst of all pinned it on someone else; but of course you do.
One sweet thing about being Catholic is that you can politely
Ask for forgiveness, and be *granted* forgiveness—I mean, *te*
Absolvo, aren't those the two most terse glorious words ever?
But the crucial part of the sacrament that we don't talk about
Is the next part, the part after you leave the church. You walk
To the river and while you are pretending to watch for herons
You envision each person against whose holiness you did sin,
And to each you apologize, and ask for forgiveness. Some of
Them are long gone from this world but not from the Infinite
Mercy who remembers all levels and forgetteth not a sparrow.
You are absolved not when a man says so but when *you* have
Asked, with every fiber of your being, to be forgiven, to walk
Home clean, to start again, to be *possible*. What we really ask
For in the sacrament of reconciliation is to be a question mark
Again, to be a verb, to be not what we did but what we might
Yet be able to do; a map of the unknown, an unfinished song.

Cill Fhíonáin

One time many years ago I was shuffling lazily in Ireland,
In County Limerick, and suddenly was running from a bull.
I kid you not. I was maundering along feeling auld soddish
And feeling like every blessed bush was my ancient cousin
And then I was running like hell from a huge furious being
Who wanted to stick his horn in my private parts. I wanted
To say something calming about being cousins in the misty
Rain or suchlike but he was, well, huge and furious. I leapt
Over a fence and kept going. He said something inarguably
Rude. I remember it was muddy as hell, and the field stank,
And the cold metal fence rattled alarmingly as I sailed over.
Only now I realize the bull had taught me a piercing lesson;
Probably everything every Irish American thinks about old
Ireland is total crap, and real Ireland is testy and possessive
And not real thrilled about visitors who don't pay attention.
Also some of it smells like shit and some is deep wet sticky
Muck from which wild and amazing beings and stories rise.
There are a lot of old fences, some of which are useful, and
Some of which ought to be torn down. The beautiful glories
Of things like bushes have savage thorns. It's unforgettable,
And savage, and not what you think, and more than it seems.

Miraculum

One day years ago a very small child said to me,
Quietly but firmly, *you are not listening to what
I am saying*, and ever after I have been trying to.
I bent down, that time, feeling shame, but it was
Too late. Words and miracles are swift and rude
And they don't wait. Often words are miraculous
And sometimes words are the flags or tendrils of
Miracles. I find that stories often have doors and
Windows through which you can see the miracle.
Miracles in my experience are not naked, and do
Not arrive with trumpet flourishes, and announce
Themselves, and register with the local authority,
Religious or civil. Miracles are in general uncivil,
In fact. Quite often they are an unholy holy mess;
The girl in the first line of the poem, for example.
I saw her arrive wetly in this world: *what* a mess!
Yet the miracle is inarguable. Many words apply,
Like *cellular mitosis*, but they're only drapery on
That which seems normal but is of course miracle.
Though, wait, there *are* naked miracles—*she* was.

On the River of Sycamores

I was in the sternum of America recently,
In country farrowed by tractors and rains
Epic and *right out of your Old Testament,*
As one man said to me, smiling a tiny bit,
And I got to talking to a man who carved
Canoes for fun, now that he was as old *as*
Anyone ever in the county that I know of,
As he said. He had been a farmer—raising
Soybeans and corn and kids, mostly. And
That's what we export just now from here,
He said, used to be the kids stayed around
But now they just don't. Mostly old ladies
Now and some old men trying to be useful
Like yours truly. I bring the canoes to kids
In schools. Perhaps if they get interested in
Rivers and fish and turtles, they might stay.
You never know. You have to be absorbed
By a place to stay when you could go. You
Have to think you'll never understand it all.
That's how I think. I bet I been on the river
As much as anybody in thousands of years,
I been on it top to bottom, in every weather
And every season, since I was a boy, which
Is a mighty long time ago, and I hardly ever
Missed a day, and I know about two percent
Of what there is to know about it, and that's
Knowledge that changes every day anyways

As the river does. I'd like kids to feel stupid
And wild curious about the river too, I guess.
That sounds selfish but I think it's crucial, if
We want to keep folks living here. If no one
Lives here, rich people will just buy the river,
And that would be an awful thing. We smile,
But you know what I mean. Someone would
Think they can close it or use it for a garbage
Dump or make it a real big sluice, or like that.
That would be an awful thing. The poor river,
It just got its otters back finally! It needs kids.
Kids on rivers: that's how rivers get into kids.

Poem After Sunday Morning Church Service in a Tent

In a huge hotel where the concierge told me there had been count them
Three weddings the day before, which is why they erected the epic tent.
I got there early and watched people file in. The tall guitar player asked
Me if I was the minister. The minister turned out to be a lady who once
She got started talking never really stopped except for the music. When
The songs started everyone except me stood and held hands and swayed.
I am a Catholic man and we only hold hands with children and we don't
Sway. I tried for a while to figure out what species of church service this
Was but you just could not tell. There was the swaying, which seemed to
Be Baptist, and discussion of sacrifice and fasts, which seemed Calvinist,
And there was talk of the Spirit and the One and suchlike, which seemed
Unitarian to me, but then I heard the name Christos . . . Greek Orthodox?
For a minute there I wondered if there would be snake-handling or maybe
A sudden burst from the Koran, or a pause while we discussed the Torah,
But the service stayed determinedly undeterminable. In the opening salvo
Of this service I was amused, thinking that it might be something offered
By the hotel for its guests, an attractant, some expensive consultant's idea
For adding value to your stay at the hotel, and I marveled at the marketing
Brilliance of it—welcoming everyone, offending no one, proffering ritual
Without a trademark, adding bonus usage to the rent of the tent, as well as
Excellent community relations. But soon I stopped being amused and was
Moved, despite the endless blather of the minister. People had come to *be*
Moved. They had come to hold hands and sing. There were bright ribbons
On the folding chairs by the aisle to signal the bride's or the groom's side.
There was a man's green tie knotted to a tent stake. There were tiny babies
In their mothers' arms. There was a man hunched in a wheelchair. Why do

We ever bother to argue about religion? All religions are the same glorious
Wine, susceptible to going bad but capable of quiet joyous gentle elevation.
They're all useful and useless, mesmerized and ruined by power but always
Pregnant with the possibility of humility. They are so easy to ignore. You'd
Be wise to sneer, with every reason imaginable for the curl of your knowing
Lip. Yet here I am, on Sunday morning, in the wedding reception tent, agog;
Not so much at the earnest idiot of a minister, but at everyone, sweetly, else.

The Other Half

The first time I shared a bed with the woman who would be my wife
Was in May, nearly thirty years ago, and I would guess that we have
Missed sharing the bed maybe a few hundred nights over those years,
What with travel and the occasional disagreements and such, but still,
That leaves us with about ten thousand nights sharing the bed, a huge
And significant number, it seems to me. We have shared the bed with
Kids and books and teacups and spectacles and once or twice the dog,
Although that is against the rules and we will not dwell further on this
For fear we will embarrass him and he will lie down facing the corner
Which he does when he feels guilty which makes us laugh, though we
Should not laugh at such a sensitive conscience . . . ten thousand nights!
And each time she was someone different, someone I hardly knew, an
Enigma wrapped in thin pajamas inside a robe the color of wilderness.
And a wilderness she has gracefully and mysteriously remained to me;
Not one of those nights did I ever know what she would say next, how
Or why she would reach for me, or even more sensually somehow, *not*
Reach for me in the way *you* are thinking, but just press up against me
Like half of something delighted to be home at last with the other half.

Bruised and Blunt

Visited a class of seventeen-year-old human beings yesterday,
And we spent an hour together talking about grace and humor
And pain and violence and stories and lies and jobs and terror
And money and pretty much everything else, and while we all
Started out somewhat polite and reserved, that didn't last, and
Soon things were open and honest, and even bruised and blunt.
I was moved. Rarely do you see tall kids unburden themselves;
Usually they peer out from behind the castle walls, or send out
Straw men to test the wind, or emerge only if draped in motley.
Maybe because I was undignified, they did not have to pretend
To be; maybe that was it, or just some twist of the wet weather.
Whatever it was that cracked their masks, out they came, some
Of them, shyly. You could almost hear their curiosity shuffling
Gently out of their quotidian disguise. Their questions were not
Questions at all, really. I think this was a new country for them,
And safe, somehow. They knew we would never see each other
Again, and I was not parent or teacher or minister or policeman;
So their questions were much more admissions and confessions
Than questions, more oblique sidelong intimacies than inquiries.
Finally the bell rang, and I suppose the most savory compliment
Is that no one moved. Then they came past and we shook hands,
Or they nodded, and two boys gently tapped me on the shoulder
With their fists, which in guy language is how you say affection,
And respect, and thank you for not being a visiting pompous ass.
I walked out so full of hope I am sure I spilled some by the door.

Poem for a Late Odd Great Odd Priest

A friend of mine died a few years ago, and his fellow priests
Buried him in a box in a lovely little oak-strewn field where
An excellent stone fence runs along the path (he loved stone
Fences, and studied them and drew them and was captivated
By the intricate engineering of them, by how patiently you'd
Have to make them, contemplating fit and angle and capacity
For bearing weight—his favorite was one in which the maker
Deliberately left spaces for chipmunks to escape from foxes),
But back on the university campus where he lived the longest
His friends quietly planted a tree in his memory; *thuja plicata*,
Western red cedar, another species of being he much admired,
Like chipmunks and foxes and students. I walk past this cedar
Every other day or so just to say hey and remember my friend.
He was the gentlest eccentricest oddest graciousest priest ever.
Students loved him, I think because he was so patently gentle;
He would never lecture anyone or even give advice. His great
Gift was just listening. He was a most excellent unsurpassable
Listener. If there was a hall of fame for listeners, he would've
Been elected on the first ballot, no question. Well, yesterday I
Wandered past his tree, and paused to enjoy the breeze sifting
Through the lacy branches of the tree (cedars play great music
On wild days), and I said hey to my friend, who was assuredly
Listening somehow, and then I noticed that someone had built
A tiny cairn of stones at the foot of the tree. Padre would have
Loved that—he would have mused that caterpillars or crickets
Built it for spiritual reasons. He would have laughed for weeks.

That Generous Minute

One time years ago I had surgery on a part of my spine I will never see.
I remember that the operating room was so bright that a nurse asked me
If I wanted to wear thin sunglasses. The surgeon was a man from Russia.
His nickname among the staff was Vlad the Impaler. He was a garrulous
Fellow. He explained everything to me carefully and then there was one
Moment or so when we just looked at each other. I was beyond terrified.
I was terrified in a whole new definition of the word terrified. It was like
Terrified and I thought we knew each other but I had just found out a lot
More about terrified and I was shocked at how I had not known terrified
Hardly at all. I started to cry. Yes, I did. A man age thirty, crying quietly.
I was afraid I would never walk again, and never make love to my lovely
New bride, and somehow be sentenced to this awful searing pain always.
And this is what I wanted to tell you: the doctor leaned down, and he put
His hand on my head, and he said quietly *I am going to do very good job.*
You do not be afraid. I am going to meticulous. You can trust me to do it.
You go to sleep and let me do my work. I love this work and I am careful
And will not rush or make mistakes. It is okay to cry. I cry too sometimes,
When I am scared of what I cannot see. You go to sleep. I will do it good.
Now usually, at the end of a poem like this, right here there would be sort
Of a conclusion, some finishing statement like *and he was right,* but that's
Not what the poem is about. It's about his calm hand and murmured grace.
Maybe he didn't mean what he said and he said stuff like that all the time,
But I don't think so. That's all I wanted to tell you—that generous minute.

The Who of Him

One time a while ago a child of mine was very sick,
And he staggered to the bathroom, and there was an
Accident, and very weakly there was a call for help,
And I found myself, fifteen years after the last time
I cleaned him, cleaning him again. Many things had
Changed since that last time, foremost among them
The fact that he was four feet taller, and that he had
Been terribly surly for a couple of years, and he had
A girlfriend now, and an attitude, and a vague future
Having something to do with rap music and old cars;
But it was startling and moving to see the things that
Had not changed at all. The washcloth, the cloud of
Powder, the stillness, the sheer stutter of amazement
At his body in the world. There was a *lot* more body
This time than there was before, but the who of him
Was still there inside all that shy skin. Even then, as
I finished and he leaned on me as he staggered back
To bed, I knew that not saying anything was exactly
The right thing to say. Sometimes the most eloquent
Words to say are those you know not to. Maybe that
Is where poems come from, shambling out of silence.

Poem in Which Jesus Christ Rolls His Ankle on the Road to Betharaba

He rolls it good, too; he wasn't paying sharp attention to the rough trail,
And he steps on a slippery rock, and down he goes, instantly aware that
This is a savage sprain. It's not like he's never blown a wheel before: he
Spent a lot of time between ages twelve and thirty sprinting and chasing
After sheep, and climbing trees, and racing his pals, and playing endless
Games that entailed spinning and dashing and whirling, so he's seen this
Instant ballooning of the joint, and the subsequent blue-and-green mottle,
And he knows there's no hope of ice, so he is basically up a creek. Many
Men right here would burst out cursing with remarkable pith and fluency,
But he knows this is not the time to call on the Chief Musician, as it says
In the Psalms; you want to save your desperate plea card for the one time
You need it most, as he will, in the Garden of Gethsemane, in three years.
Which he knows, just as he knows he'll be sagging on a cross—he's seen
It all, and not just in his dreams at night but sometimes suddenly at dawn,
Or at suppertime; his mom recognizes the signs, and makes him lie down.
And all this is why he starts laughing, right there in the dust, as he notices
The ankle achieve a little of the lurid yellow color that follows blue-green.
He could just touch it and all would be well; he could command the crows
To lift him breezily to Betharaba, where he will call his first five disciples;
He could, if he chose, ask the very stones that brought him down to sculpt
Themselves into carts and mules, into granitic eagles, into miraculous boats
Of the purest rock; but that would be poor form, as he says aloud, grinning.
That would blow the whole script, the whole genius of the thing, the entire
Book of Revolution as written; and I will not muddle that which my father
Has made clear to me among all the children of his love. So up he staggers,
Awfully tempted to curse again, for there's no pain quite like a really badly

Sprained ankle; you are quite sure you will never walk normally again. But He cuts a stick from a bush, apologizing gently to the plant for the damage, And thanking it for the loan of a member, and off he limps to his incredible Fate; but to give him his immense due, he lumbers along laughing. He who Will salve the sins of the world, and open the door eternally for forgiveness, And bring all willing beings home to the unimaginable but ubiquitous Love: *That* guy sprains his ankle so badly it looks like he's wearing a pumpkin on His foot? *That* guy shambles along, laughing? Astonishingly, yes—that guy.

Tell Me Tell Me Tell Me

I board the airplane to see my parents. They live far away and long ago
And some years into the future; you never met such wry time machines
In your life. Sometimes they will be about to pass the marmalade when
Suddenly it is late 1941 and they are in college and kissing on the train;
But then as you slather your toast it is 1967 and a war wants to eat their
Son or 2012 and they are at that son's wake or 1929 and a father comes
Home without his job, or it is a week ago, and do you think that Federer
Is the finest tennis player ever, or Laver, or Don Budge? It happens that
Fast. It's unnerving and glorious and confusing and perfect and I would
Sit with them every afternoon, if I could, and say tell me tell me tell me,
Tell me every moment of your whole lives, don't leave me here without
Your grace and humor and the extraordinary gleaming jar of marmalade
From which come all your stories. *Next year in Ireland . . .* says my mother,
And my dad grins, and I want to kneel and beg the Lord for this moment
Again and again always, the inarguable yes of their bodies, the resonance
Of their endurance, the hunch and hollow of their shoulders, the reverent
Geography of their faces, the lean song of my father's hands on the table.

Poem for a Friend Whose Sister Died Monday at Dusk

An older sister; and that is everything we need to know
For the few lines of this poem, because her olderness is
Her rocking his crib when he was just born, and her not
Punching him out when he deliberately scissored a skirt
Of hers when he was furious about something, and how
She held him and rocked him when their dad died, even
Though by then he was much taller and stronger. Let us
Keep that embrace in mind as a way to pray for her now,
Her face nestled up against his neck and he is sobbing &
They both can feel the throb of the blood they share. Let
Them stand there for a long time. We think time passeth
And flees into the past but this is not so. There is no past
As long as there are stories. Stories are how we embrace
Each other whether we can touch each other or not; trust
Me on this. I have so often been wrong, but not this time.

Who We Are

I was in a kindergarten recently and I
Handed a child a blank sheet of paper
And asked him to write down his life,
And I expected him to draw a map or
Write something down or draw a face
Or jot down numbers or sketch music,
But he laughed, and held the paper up
Over his face. I think his message was
That we are always being written, and
That which we think are nouns are not;
But then he crumpled and ate the sheet,
Which perhaps means it's always time
To eat. A while later, though, I noticed
Him making a bear from wet red paper.
You never saw such a lovely wondrous
Bear made out of spit and a former tree
In your life. As I was leaving I saw him
Give it to another kid, who was thrilled.
It is the startling wry minutes like these
That write who we are. Every time you
Are rammed by joy; isn't that your life?

Times Tables

Just got a note from my mom, in which she tells me
That my gentle wry witty subtle sister, now resident
In a monastery, used to rock my cradle with her foot
While chanting her multiplication tables aloud. How
I would love to report that I remember every blessed
Moment of this, how my sister tried to achieve a sort
Of whispered chant (loud enough to be articulate but
Soft enough not to wake me), how my mother would
Forget about us and get absorbed by heated table talk
About religions and wars and then realize with a start
That my sister was on her seventeenth run-through of
Her times tables, how my dad would smile and say O
Let her rip for another hour and the both of them will
Be math geniuses! But I don't remember . . . do I? Now
That I think about it, I worship rhythm and measure it
Unconsciously, automatically—I have an extra ear for
The cadence of crows, the coughing of motors, an owl
Calling sixteen times to another, who calls back seven:
And seven times sixteen equals a way to spell out love.

Poem for Miss Mary MacKillop, of Fitzroy

Today's startling news: Australia's only recognized Catholic saint,
So far, was born on Brunswick Street, in Fitzroy! Now, you might
Wonder why this is an astonishing bit of ironic and amazing news,
If you have never been to Fitzroy, a rough neighborhood in the tall
Old seething roaring city of Melbourne—but I have been there and
I can tell you that Fitzroy always was and will be a wry wilderness;
Every color and ethnicity and language you can imagine lives there.
I am not kidding. The commission flats, the dogleg brooding alleys,
The trams—I walked there for weeks and saw every kind of sad and
Cruel and lost and tough and gentle and graceful and awful and holy
There is, seems to me—I saw a lot of Australia in twenty city blocks.
And now I see wee quiet shy Mary MacKillop there, minding a shop.
She is fourteen. Her people are Scottish. She will be legendary, later,
For her ferocious dedication to helping the poor—you cannot ignore
Them, she will say one million times to power and money and pomp.
You cannot pretend you do not see them. You cannot say that we are
A great and lucky country when so many innocents are starving. You
Can lie to yourself and in public but I will not lie also. Look at all the
Huddled souls, raped and beaten and hungry and cold. They are all us.
Yes, they are. This has nothing to do with religion and class. They are
All us. If there is a great Australia it will be the one that rises to house
And feed and protect those who have nothing. I saw them when I was
A child on Brunswick Street and now I can't not see them. Thousands
Of them in every city and county and state and reserve. They're all us.
The whole country is Brunswick Street. Come with me to pick one up.

Drunks I Have Known

A wonderful storyteller I liked very much, and when he passed
One of his friends said *John Barleycorn* when a mourner asked
What illness carried him off. A woman I knew who said herself
Bluntly that she wanted to be so drunk so fast every morning so
She would forget her father's name and face because he was the
Devil. A man I met once who said he had never had a drop until
He was near thirty and the first drop was an ocean that lasted ten
Years and killed every bit of love and it's taken me twenty years
To try to get it to tiptoe back in my direction now that I am sober.
I listen to the stories and wince and pray and pour myself another
Glass—carefully. The one leads to six without you even noticing,
A man said to me once. One is fun and two is twice, he said, then
You should stop and get up and do the laundry and have some tea.
Laundry saved my life, I think. Launderers Anonymous, that's me.

Some Sort of a Prayer

I gave a rambling talk recently and a long line of teenagers came
Up to speak to me afterward and it was instantly clear that every
Single one of them wanted to ask me something while ostensibly
Asking me something else, or say one thing while seeming to say
Something else. I was so instantly moved I could hardly stammer
Any sort of answer. I tried hard to hear what they were not saying
Aloud but *were* saying with remarkable courage. It takes startling
Courage to be a teenager, you know. There are so many theatrical
Personas to try, but masks and disguises can get stuck. Or you get
Trapped behind walls that begin as protective but become prisons.
One kid in particular stays with me. He's tall and shy and nervous.
He says *How do you deal with rejection?* and somehow I instantly
Get it that he does not mean essays and stories and poems and how
You handle people saying steadily bluntly no to your insistent yes!
He's asking me about hope and despair and lovers and heartbreaks.
He's asking about the girl or boy he adores who does not love him.
He's staring at me. The other kids wait politely. I want to reach up
And cup his face in my hands as if he was my son, but you have to
Be honest with kids, you cannot merely bloviate and issue arrogant
Pomposity, so I tell him you have to learn to be neighborly with no.
You are going to see it every day and you might as well be friendly
With the concept. Someone else's no doesn't actually kill your yes;
It only means that someone else's yes is still out there waiting. You
See where I am going here? There's more yes than no, is what I am
Trying to say. I suppose that's what we mean by faith. Faith's a big
Word, bigger than any religion. It means yes where everything sure

Looks like no as far as you can see. Am I making the slightest sense
Here, son? I actually call him son. The other kids must have thought
I was being avuncular but for a brief moment he was indeed my son,
And yours too. We shook hands and he held onto my hands just a bit
Longer than the usual thing, which I took to be some sort of a prayer.

A Note on the Apostles

Thought: if we estimate, conservatively, that about ten percent
Of any group is gay, and there were twelve apostles, that means
That at least one of them was gay—which means, if we adhere
To the same reasoning that says we can only have male priests
Because all the apostles were male, that we must have one gay
Priest in every group of twelve. This leads to all sorts of issues.
What if there are no gay candidates, does one of the others have
To act as if he was gay? What would that entail? The reasoning
Of the whole priesthood thing is interesting; if we really did this
Right, we would choose only short Jewish men from the Levant,
And require that they be fluent in not only Hebrew but Aramaic.
But back to the gay apostle—Matthew, who ever so generously
Invited Jesus to dinner? One of the fishermen? John, who Jesus
Loved the best? Peter, married but struggling with commitment?
Philip, who loved horses? Simon the Zealot, who maybe erected
A violent tempestuous self because he was grappling with sexual
Identity? Who knows? I mean, Jesus never did marry, and He did
Love John, and Mary Magdalene sure seems to have had a crush
On Him, and He was so gentle and polite with her, in just the way
A gay gentleman would be honest enough to courteously decline
A chance to pursue romance with someone of another orientation.
But who's to say? And, ever so gently, I'd like to say, who cares?

Why Do You Bother to Write Poems?

Is the question from the back of the room; I cannot
Quite see the student asking it, but it's deep-voiced
And challenging and I assume it's a guy. Because I
Want to rub music and language together and gawk
At the flames, I say. Because poetry, if it takes fire,
Cracks people's masks, and assaults arrogance, and
Sucks you beneath the surface of words toward why
We use them. Because we have been singing before
There *were* words and it's healthy to remember that.
Because the great poems are about you and me both
And there is damned little we will be able to discuss
In the normal flow of the river and it's good for both
Of us to stand together quietly for a while in a poem.
Because why the hell not? What is it exactly that we
Should count as time better spent? You cannot spare
Two minutes for a poem? Sure, it might be pompous
Arty muck, and you demand your two minutes back,
But what if it isn't? What if it shivers you, or startles
You awake, or makes you weep remembering a time
When you sang all day too, and everything was made
Of music and light and colors and slabs of shimmer?
What if, brother—that's my answer to your question.

What Happens After You Die?

Asks a moppet of perhaps eight years old, in a class
That was supposed to be religious but which soared
Much deeper than the traditional caper and frippery.
I know what I am supposed to say, being the teacher.
I am supposed to use words like *god* and *heaven* and
Peace and *light*. But I find that I cannot just bloviate,
Not today, not this girl, not any wild holy frightened
Child, and we are all this kid all the time, are we not?
No one has the slightest idea, I say. Whatever you're
Told in no uncertain terms is a whopping lie. But I'd
Suggest that we consider these interesting hints. One:
There was never a you before and there will never be
An exactly you ever again; you are a once-only offer.
Do you think such a prize would be allowed to easily
Expire? Think about it. Two: no energy is lost, as we
Recall from our discussion of the miracle of What Is.
So the energy that is you can't be lost after the vessel
In which you are currently poured is broken. You are
More than the hall in which you are currently housed.
Think about it. Three: all things have to morph forms.
That's a basic rule from the Imagineer—but changing
Form doesn't mean you are not you anymore. Look at
Yourselves just from last year to this year. Liam alone
Is four inches taller, so his *form* has changed, but he is
Still himself, is he not? Which is a mixed blessing, but
Let's not get distracted. Just think about that. Also you
Might as well bet on the chance of miracles far beyond

Our understanding happening after we die. Why not go
For it? What do you have to lose? If there are miracles
Far beyond our understanding *now*, like mule deer and
Kestrels and sunfish and willows and every one of you,
Not to mention the miracle of such as me pretending to
Be your teacher, why could there not be miracles later?
Maybe miracles are *thrilled* that you are in a new form,
Couldn't that be? Think about it. Four: it might be that
After we die we all go to something like Hawaii, which
Would be awesome, wouldn't it? Let's think about *that*
For three whole minutes. Yes, you can sing if you want,
And then what say we let class out early today, singing?

Poem for My Friend Shoshana

Who opens the mail I send her at the dining room table,
She told me once, and she reads it aloud to her husband,
And they grin, I hope, and probably something reminds
Them of something in their long wild holy-headed lives,
And they talk about it for a bit, and then there is perhaps
Tea. Sometimes when I drop my letters in the mail I can
See the tablecloth and smell the tea and see the oak trees
Out in the street, the burl of the legs of the wooden table.
What tales the table could tell! The weeping, the hilarity;
The long afternoons, the pile of mail, the old silver letter
Opener that belonged to a granddad. Our smallest things
Are us, don't you think? The favorite pencil, the tea mug
You use because your daughter's blessed lips loved it for
All those years. The spoons you choose above the others.
We age, we grow weary, we worry, we grin, we stare out
At the oak trees, we are thirty, we are eighty, there is one
Letter this morning that does not ask for money. In a few
Minutes I will print out this poem, and fold it, and scrawl
The word *love* in my usual tiny illegible scribble and fold
It into an envelope and off it goes through various offices
With whirring machinery and men cursing cheerfully and
In three days it will be across the country and in her hand,
And she will read it to Bernie, and we take all this so very
Much for granted, don't we? The mail, the urge to make a
Poem, the table, the tea, the oaks, the easy patient warmth
Of a friend. Friends are the clans we belong to by accident
Of place and space and grace. What a gift, such a seeming
Chance: could such a pleasure really be just happenstance?

What It Is You Would
Like the Stone to Say

Called the cemetery this morning to begin to plot
What happens to my mom and dad after they die.
Yes, I just wrote *plot*. My parents would smile at
That. They are not afraid. They have lived so wry
And well. They survived wars and four dead sons
And savage diseases, and they still reach for each
Other here and there. I have seen it. The cemetery
People are so very helpful. Discharge papers: that
Is the first thing. The cemetery will donate a head
Stone free of charge. And the casket liner. I admit
The casket liner was not on my list of stuff to talk
To the cemetery folks about. Plenty of room, says
The cemetery lady. Yes, your mom will be buried
With your dad, no charge. What do we engrave on
The stone? The specific words? *In loving memory,*
Usually. That is standard. Can you edit the words?
Well, I suppose so. Within reason. There are space
Concerns, of course. I suggest you talk to your dad
And mom and brothers and sisters, and agree upon
What it is you would like the stone to say. I would
Like the stone to say grace, and sinewy, and young.
They were so young when they married. He did not
Expect to survive the war. Their first son died—his
Name was Seamus. Can you find room for Seamus
On the stone? Mom nearly died, too. But she is too
Tough to die at thirty. A hundred and thirty, maybe.

Can we say endurance, and prayerful, and compose
A poem about how they like their tea, and who gets
What section of the paper first, and how they never
Ever forget a birthday or anniversary? Can we copy
Their meticulous undamaged handwriting? Can you
Show the note of her laughter, and the way he never
Misses a day with the crossword and how he is right
Now bending over the tomato plants to be sure he is
Not about to water the tiny shy frogs who live there?

The *Solving* of Prose

Now, if you are like me, which God forbid . . .
No, no, I have used that line before, & more
Than once, too. Am I all done with words at
Last? Have my cheerful companions of fifty
Years fled finally? Oh, I remember when we
Met, I remember every taste of the dawning
Pleasures: My sister read to me after dinner,
And I heard words as a sort of gentle music;
You know what I mean. All the other family
Voices woven and murmuring. The splayed
Newspapers. Words *did* whisper to me: I am
Not kidding. I liked to stare at them. Puzzles
On parade, and so mannerly, lined up just so,
Margin to margin. I don't remember learning
To read, or the instant when it all broke open,
But I do vividly remember being *able* to read,
And being thrilled, and reading hungrily, and
Being amazed that I was never too full. There
Were so many tastes, too, and always another
Code to crack. We forget the sheer delight of
Reading, the *solving* of prose—that shy thrill
Of finding for yourself what had been strewn
On the page as clues. Then of course a zillion
Other pleasures, like writing, and dabbling in
Other languages, and reading to my own kids,
But those are all the province of other poems;
Let's stay in that first hour that you learned to

Read. Wasn't that one of the best hours ever?
Wouldn't it be cool to catch a glimpse of that
Hour now, and burst out laughing at the child
Darting around the house opening every book,
With a smile bigger than all of Burkina Faso?

My Track Career

Yes, I ran track in high school. Although for me
It was more like sprinting madly and then trying
Not to barf between sprints. I remember the first
Practice very well indeed. The coach asked us if
We were runners or sprinters. You could hear an
Epic moral distinction between the words; coach
Loved distance men and tolerated *the fast-twitch*
Guys, as he called us. I chose to sprint. The other
Sprinters and I were sent to the remote end of the
Field, to work out on our own. The distance guys
Took off with coach on a nice easy nine-mile run.
We sprawled in the grass, talking. A guy smoked
A cigarette and then offered the pack around. We
Decided to run a few sprints just for fun. One guy
Did barf. No one said anything, though. I thought
That was pretty cool, that no one ragged him. We
Saw an osprey with what looked like a small bass.
The next part of this poem probably ought to chat
About the actual sprinting, and whether I did well
Or not, and how we did as a team, but what I love
Best about my obscure track career was this hour,
Sprawled in the scrawny grass, gawking at osprey,
And being secretly pleased that no one had razzed
The guy who barfed. Perhaps I wouldn't be teased
Either, for not being a particularly speedy sprinter.
And the prospect of not being ragged for not being
Great, while also having the chance to see osprey?
Well—I report with pleasure it was a *great* season.

The Alcove Wall on the West Side of Alumni Hall at the University of Notre Dame: A Note

A student asks me about my own college experience
And for some odd entertaining reason the first image
That rises from the inexhaustible ocean of memories
Is feeble sunlight on a sandstone wall. The courtyard
Wall of a dormitory. But the yard was tiny and moist
And mostly shadowed and no one ever cut through it
Or sprawled or slept or wept or puffed or prayed in it,
Except me, of course. I liked it because it was so lost.
And not because I felt a kinship: I reveled in my time,
And delighted in new friends, and got a running start
On the shape and song of my life. But I sure liked the
Little muddy courtyard, and made a point of stopping
By it as often as possible during my years in that hall.
The scraggly bushes, the uneven grass, the admirable
Humility of the wall, which had no architectural flair,
No engraved wise remark, no stony saints, no granite
Escutcheon, no subtle cross or lily or rose or rampant
Beast of prey. It was a working wall, which I came to
Appreciate very much. The day I graduated I stopped
By the courtyard just to say hey, and there was a shaft
Of feeble sunlight on the wall, which made me happy
For reasons I cannot quite explain. The wall looked so
Painterly, so patient, so dignified—a little light makes

Such a difference. It sounds odd to report that I strode
Away feeling like I was leaving something important,
But I *did* feel that way. Now imagine the scene where
I try to explain all this to the dazed inquisitive student.

Mao's Socks

He must have worn socks, am I right?
Because it's stunningly cold in China,
And even Mao couldn't execute winter.
And he must have put them on himself,
Because having a flunky do it would be
Bad form according to Party principles,
Although if ever there was a tyrant who
Flouted the principle of all for one and
One for all it was Mao, who murdered
Maybe forty million of his compatriots.
But let's get back to his socks. He's no
Pixie in his later years, so he must have
Put them on with a laborious grunt, like
Any older portly guy. But socks, that's
A basic everyday everybody adventure,
You know? So here's my question: did
He ever, even once, while trying to get
His socks on, and privately thinking he
Sure could lose thirty pounds, consider
Anyone and everyone else putting their
Socks on? Did he? Because how could
You casually slaughter people who are
Just like you, who find one purple sock
But not the other, who have to make an
Effort to get their socks on because you
Are more planetary than you used to be?
Just once, if he suddenly thought about

Everyone else in the nation that minute
Struggling into their socks and listening
Half-awake for the teakettle, and trying
To remember where in heaven's names
That damned other sock could possibly
Be, wouldn't he have found murder just
A bit more difficult? It's easier when no
One has a name, and they are all figures
Someone lied about. It's got to be harder
When they slump there, about to be shot
Or starved, and you look down and spot
One blue sock and one purple sock. You
Would have to laugh. Because you have
Been there too—in fact you *are* that guy.
Can you murder a man you know is you?
Poor old fat Mao: Time murdered him in
His turn. Is he wearing his socks in hell?

An Ode to Night-Tables

Which we all have, or had, or will have; you had one
As a child, and never noticed its sturdy patient maple
Character, though you slept so near to it for ten years
Or more, and it held your books, your reading lamps,
The glass of water your mom never forgot to provide.
Later when you lived on your own you had to go buy
Or borrow one, and this was the first time you stared
At the actual thing, and noted its spindly strength, its
Predilection to utility; not so many night-tables boast
Ornatery, the mass of them dodging every pretension.
They are made to serve and not to show; to work, not
To speak of class or ambition thereto, or shout money.
No one ever exclaims over them at the cocktail soiree;
No weekend carpenter runs an appreciative hand over
The deft plane and polish. Most of their lives they are
Alone, with only the bed and the bureau for company;
And even in the evening, when the bed is occupied, &
The light is beaming, and someone lifts a book off the
Night-table, and the alarm clock is rewound, and their
Spectacles are folded and laid on the acquiescent pine,
Does anyone savor the table for an instant, and ponder
The virtue of patience? No; but maybe tonight we will.

Life Is a Hospital in Which Every Patient Is Haunted by the Desire to Change Beds

Is a line from the poet Baudelaire, and I beg to differ.
Listen, *haunted* is a heavy word there, Charles me lad.
I would go with *niggled*, or *bothered*, or every once in
A while you suddenly think what if I hadn't broken up
With that girl, would I be in insurance today, or in jail,
Or deceased, in a legendary washing-machine mishap?
But you can't live in the land of what might have been,
Brother. Which is why I quibble with *haunted*. It's not
That we're locked into the shape of our lives; certainly
Not, and you above all folks knew that we don't hardly
Control an hour of it, let alone the arc of the long story.
We do the best we can with the cards we are dealt, and
Piss and moan and dicker with the dealer. That's where
My hospital is, brother. At some point you agree to say
Yes rather than maybe. You with me here? And lest we
Lose the other intimation of your line, let's speak blunt
About life as a hospital. It's a fair metaphor. There's so
Much pain and grief and loss and surgery and the price,
Brother, the price, the cost overruns, the endless forms!
But it's a gift, my friend. It is an awfully *confusing* gift,
Yes. So unfair, so unjust, such cruelty, such an accident
Of gender and skin and place dictating so much of what
Bed you get in the hospital. When I was younger I wept

And roared at the muddle; how could life be so glorious
And so horrendous at once, sometimes, often, to the one
Person? How could my parents be such gracious humble
Souls and have four of their sons die? How could a total
Innocent be raped in [choose your own hell-name here]?
Answer: I haven't the faintest idea, and no appeals to an
Epic and unattainable God yield any sort of explanation.
Which I personally think is smart on the Unimaginable's
Part—if life made sense we'd try to commodify the poor
Thing, as we do with everything else, from sex to poetry.
But listen, we are coming to the end of this conversation,
And what I am saying is that I don't want to switch beds.
Not at all. Now, this is probably because I'm lots luckier
Than you, and you never got to chat up my subtle spouse,
Whose bearing and gestures are fair as a fair countryside,
And if somehow you *had* been granted the chance to end
Up in a most puzzling and stimulating marriage with her,
You'd agree with me that switching beds would be crazy
Talk. But we totally agree on the hospital thing, although
I think you mean untrammeled brokenness, and I believe
That hospitals and life have extraordinary grace rambling
Through the halls and showing up where you least expect
Them to be. But hey, let's get a second glass of wine, and
Maybe turn the conversation toward basketball or oysters,
Speaking of extraordinary things. Let us savor this instant
When we are together in the hospital, Charles, my brother.

If You Could Do Anything Else, What Would You Choose?

Given another interest, or absorption, in life, asks a student
In the high school, what is it you would choose? And don't
Think about it—just blurt out whatever leaps to your mouth.
Otter observer! I say, and perhaps half of the students laugh,
But the others look puzzled. Bear expert! Bassoon maestro!
Cartoonist! Trumpeter in a ska band playing the early stuff!
Professional badger herder! The guy who brings radio back
As the coolest media ever! Editor of a magazine about jays!
He who banishes despair with a touch of his left forefinger!
He who miraculously hears yes again every afternoon when
He sends his request to be married through the holy ether to
One woman in particular! And there I pause, just as startled
As the kids at what has jumped out, and then, unforgettably,
A few kids start to applaud, and then a few more. Afterward
One shy girl says to me I sure hope I meet a boy who thinks
Like that about the woman he thinks about, and I said I hope
So too and he thinks about you, and we shook hands and she
Slipped away, and the next kid says to me, sir, really, otters?

The Kid with the Blankets

A cold snap this morning, frost on the cars,
And I remembered the merchant in Chicago
Who, when it got to be twenty degrees or so,
Would silently send a boy out with blankets
For the guys huddled in the alleys for maybe
A two-block radius. I saw this happen. What
Struck me powerfully was that the kid didn't
Even ask. The boss just nodded and away he
Went, the kid with the blankets. The kid told
Me later he collected the blankets back when
The temperature went back up over freezing.
Once a year the dry-cleaner around the block
Washed the blankets for nothing. Things like
This just seem to be everything. There's a lot
Of stuff like this. There is more stuff like this
Than anyone could ever measure; maybe that
Is another reason we need God, to keep track.

In the Old Methodist Church on Vashon Island

I read aloud from my headlong prose the other night
In a gentle old wooden church on an island and then
People wanted me to sign books and such but I have
Learned that mostly they do not want my scribble as
Much as they want to *say* something to me. So often
What they have to say is quiet and haunting and just
Enough of their deepest self that you both just stand
There startled and quiet for an instant with that story
Between you like it slid out without any forethought;
A sort of jail break where you cannot believe you've
Actually made it outside the walls. So this happened,
And I stood there with this guy and his long-lost son,
And neither of us said a word, and I bet we stood for
A minute with the boy between us. He would be five
Years old now, and he would be sleepy, and I would
Goof him and ask him if he was going to have a beer
Before he went to bed and he would shyly say nooo!,
And we would all smile and then his dad would sling
Him on his shoulder and he and I would shake hands,
The dad using his left hand so he didn't drop the boy,
And I would turn politely to the next reader and offer
To deface their book. I guess what I wanted to say to
You here is that this did not happen but it did happen.
For a moment there was the little boy behind his dad,
Shy and sleepy and clutching his dad's Sunday pants.
For a minute there was a kid who was and isn't but is.

Cornerness

If all you had was a corner you were living lucky,
Says a shy gentle guy I meet in the social ramble.
It does not matter where the corner was. Ecuador,
Edmonton, Eritrea, Englewood Cliffs New Jersey.
All those places have corners for the children who
Are lucky enough to find a corner. I often wonder
About children who did not and do not find warm
Corners. Would you look for that all your life? So
No matter how warm and safe your house, you've
Always got to keep an eye out for the next corner?
I gave my corner to my sister when she was seven.
She needed it more than I did then. I had stored up
Cornerness, you might say. There is your word for
The day—that thing which makes a child feel safe.

Finbar's Party

A friend of ours celebrated his birthday in a battered barn
The other night, and it was sweet and funny, with his two
Small grandchildren flittering around, and lots of salmon,
And stuff people made and brought and laid out in dishes,
And there was a stove that everyone tried to edge toward,
Jockeying courteously just to get two minutes to thaw out,
And there were lots of odd funny conversations, and folks
Seeing each other after long years, and a *lot* of hugging of
The celebrant, and people sang, and there was a whopping
Cake, but oddly the moment I will remember best was one
In which nothing happened. The celebrant was standing in
A corner alone for a minute, with his hands in his pockets,
And the look on his face was some lovely mix of affection
And sadness and merriment and weariness and amusement
That seemed like a story or a song of who the man really *is*,
You know what I mean? Sometimes your face is the honest
Unadorned unfiltered you. It was cool to see. It did not last
More than a few seconds. The event swirled him right back
Into itself and coffee and laughter and brief funny speeches,
But for a second there was the man's whole life on his face.
This guy worked his ass off to mill what skill he had for the
Shard of holy and possible in people. He did. I saw it. A lot
Of people saw it. All you can say to a guy who worked that
Hard is thanks, man. You want another piece of berry cake?

God

By purest chance I was out in our street when the kindergarten
Bus mumbled past going slow and I looked up just as all seven
Kids on my side of the bus looked at me and I grinned and they
Lit up and all this crap about God being dead and where is God
And who owns God and who hears God better than whom is the
Most egregiously stupid crap imaginable because if you want to
See God and have God see you and have this mutual perception
Be completely untrammeled by blather and greed and comment,
Go stand in the street as the kindergarten bus murmurs past. I'm
Not kidding and this is not a metaphor. I am completely serious.
Everyone babbles about God but I saw God this morning just as
The bus slowed down for the stop on Maple Street. God was six
Girls and one boy with a bright green and purple stegosaurus hat.
Of course God would wear a brilliantly colored tall dinosaur hat!
If you were the Imagination that dreamed up everything that ever
Was in this blistering perfect terrible world, wouldn't you wear a
Hat celebrating some of the wildest most amazing developments?

A Basketball Poem

Someone says to me with honest surprise You really think
Basketball is by far the greatest of all sports? Why is that?
And out pour the answers: Because it is graceful and fluid,
And you cannot ever stop moving or anticipating or seeing
What might happen, and because the coach doesn't control
The game really at all, and because mass and height are not
The ultimate arbiters of quality, and because wit and brains
And quick and liquid speed trump burl and brawn. Because
A small skinny guy can easily fake out a big muscular dude.
Because anyone can learn to shoot the thing by shooting ten
Thousand shots alone. You can't learn football and baseball
By yourself. Basketball rewards the slight and bespectacled,
The witty and the creative, the dreamers, the ones who want
To share the ball, the ones who savor the unique geometries
Of every game. Every other sport is either war or slow chess
But basketball is neither. Basketball is rivers, and serpentine
Squiggles, and humor in motion; basketball is a sinewy verb.
Basketball is American through and through, with all the tall
Ambition and insistent energy and smiling inter-independent
Character of the country in its bones. It is theater. It is a fight
Without wounds and horror. You can sin, but only five times,
After which you are exiled from the river and can only watch.
Also there is no armor. The players are unadorned. The judge
Played the game and knows all the ways to cheat and whistles
Loud as hell when he sees sin. The field of play is good wood.

Even though official time trickles down to zero, just as in life,
A game can be extended again and again and again. In theory,
A basketball game could go into overtime forever. It might be
That this is what heaven actually is. Did I miss anything? No?

You Never Know

Driving to work this morning I saw a burly redtailed hawk
Sitting on a light pole right next to three pigeons. I craned
My head to be sure I was seeing what you would not think
You would ever see, but there they were, a whopping grim
Eater of pigeons and three pigeons whom you would think
Would be anywhere but there. But there they were. I drove
On, more slowly. I could see them in my rear-view mirror.
Whatever you think you will never see, of course you will.
Why they were perched so peaceably together is a mystery.
Perhaps the hawk had just eaten the three pigeons' cousins
And was not at all hungry, and the pigeons knew Old Hank
Was too stuffed to growl or budge. Or perhaps the pigeons
Were telling the hawk a story so amazing that the hawk had
Promised and sworn and vowed to not rip up the storyteller.
Or maybe the hawk wanted to rejigger the whole prey thing
And move toward more of a nuts and seeds dietary program.
Or maybe the hawk was an illuminated being not especially
Interested in shredding now. Or a pigeon was mesmerizing,
And this was only one of very many hawks to change sides.
You never know. Maybe the hawk was apprenticed in some
Interesting way, or working off an indentured period. Or all
Four of them had conspired to goof the human beings today.
Maybe they had gathered on the pole twelve seconds before
I shot past it, and as soon as I was gone they lost it laughing
And bowed and said we really must do this again sometime
And off they went to meetings or laundry or to their offices.
You never know. For all we know we do not know so much.

Your Secret Language

Saw two hawks courting this afternoon, over a river,
And after fifty years of raptormania I know the clans
Well enough to note that these were Cooper's hawks.
They jostle and fence and dicker and harry and whirl
For a while, and then a redtail saunters into the scene
And for some reason makes a sudden run at the male
Cooper's, upon which the female spins astonishingly
And drives the bully off with such rage that I ducked,
Down below, watching this. Then the little hawks go
Back to dickering about who should ask the other for
A dance, or whose turn it is to snag dinner, or if they
Should try to have one last kid, or whatever it is they
Were nattering about, up there, over the old oak trees.
These things are always happening, aren't they? And
We only see a tiny fraction of them, and they are wry
And perfect and terrible and everything for which we
Have no words, really. I used to be greedy—I wanted
To see and hear *everything*. I wanted to be god. I did.
Now I just want to invent songs for the few miracles
I am allowed to see. There will come a day when I'm
Incapable of words, probably; the apt fate for writers.
I've always been terrified of that—to be sentenced to
Being mute, in such a glinting merry sea of sentences.
But now I think I would be happy to watch the hawks
Whirling and dickering and jostling in the transparent
Sea of the air. Just to see them. The seeing is a lovely
Word all by itself. We hardly ever admit we are alive.
Whatever reminds you of that is your secret language.

Ash Wednesday

Here's your Ash Wednesday story.
A mother carries her tiny daughter
With her as she gets ashed and the
Girl, curious and wriggly, squirms
Into the path of the priest's thumb
Just as the finger is about to arrive
On the mother's forehead, and the
Ashes go right in the kid's left eye.
She starts to cry, and there's a split
Second as the priest and the mother
Gawk, and then they both burst out
Laughing. The kid is too little to be
Offended, and the line moves along,
But this stays with me; not the ashy
Eye as much as the instant when all
Could have been pain and awkward
But instead it led to mutual giggling.
We are born of star-dirt and dreams,
And unto this we shall return, that is
The Law, but meantime, by God, we
Can laugh our asses off. What a gift,
You know? Let us snicker while we
Can, brothers and sisters. Let us use
That which makes dark things quail.

On a Basketball Court in Atlanta

One more tiny story that isn't tiny about my late
Brother Kevin who sure wasn't tiny either being
Well over six feet tall and roughly an eighth of a
Ton as I loved to say to him if I was away across
The room and safe from his arm as long as today.

One time we were playing basketball at a college
In Georgia, the usual eclectic pickup game where
Some guys were deft and other guys thought they
Were and some were just getting in their workout
And others were working out their egos and there

Was a scuffle under the boards and a guy starts in
On me but my brother *looms* hugely—establishes
The inarguable fact of his grim largeness, an *I am
Here* statement with which no guy could disagree,
And that was that. Some people speak articulately

Without words. He was really good at that. People
Thought him curt and gruff and stern but I thought
He said a lot in other ways. Faces speak, of course,
And our hands, and the way we loom and duck, or
Stand up, or don't. He stood up. I don't forget that.

Easter Morning

A flurry of shoes; the last time some of them were worn
Was Christmas, or at the wake where the fistfight broke
Out between drunken uncles. The ceremonial complaint
About the tightness of the tie. That was a haunting wake.
There was keening. Keening is wailing that frightens off
The evil spirits. Lucifer marshals them. He was an angel.
He fell from grace. So might we all. The uncles fell thus.
The police had to intervene. Grandmother was mortified.
Grandfather would have loved every blessed minute of it,
Uncle Jack says. He would, so. He lived with a high roar.
Lucifer squirms in agony on Easter. Aunt Aileen says so.
Her name means light in Gaelic. The oldies speak Gaelic
When they want to talk about the most interesting things.
Uncle Jack says Granddad would have leapt into the fray
Roaring with a vibrant joy now vanished from the world.
You will not see the like of that man again. There's only
The one of him. Like your man Jesus. The poor fella had
No wake! Don't mention this to your aunt. That poor lad.
Can you imagine the roar at His wake, now? The apostles
At the keening and the women louder and angels in ranks
Beyond measure. No Lucifer, no; he'd be too bitter. He'd
Stay home all savage at the death of his enemy. You need
A good enemy to be your best self, boys. So now imagine
Lucifer's shock and mixed emotion when the Lord arises!
His greatest general, Death, has been defeated, but his one
Most bitter irrevocable enemy is totally back in the game!
Now, that's why we go to Mass this morning, boys. Never

You miss Easter Mass, for it's the anniversary of a terrific
Victory in a battle that's been waged over billions of years.
Still is, boys, still is. You'll play your part. Never forget it.
You miss Easter Mass, boys, and Lucifer smiles his awful
Smile, all stench and despair. Fight him, boys! Now, don't
Be telling your aunt about this chat, as she has theological
Ideas firm as the pillars of Hercules. Right. Handkerchiefs,
Dollar each for the collection, shoes tied? Boys, we're off.

On All Souls Day

All my life, when I thought about death coming for me,
I wondered *how* he would come, and what costumes he
Would wear (cancer coat? stroke suits?), and if I would
Be a weenie, whining all the way to the end, or die wry,
Smiling a bit and offering dry and entertaining remarks,
But now I think I know myself well enough to know I'll
Be seriously *interested* in the whole thing. Can you chat
With death, is that possible? Can you, you know, natter?
I am not kidding. Every death is a whole new way to die.
My stroke will be unlike Robert Louis Stevenson's—not
Just because he was younger or in Samoa or a lot thinner,
But because I am made of love and song and amusement
In ways he was not and could not know. My death is new
Country not just for me but for my death. I feel a passing
Empathy for my death—it only gets the one shot at doing
What it is designed to do. We are weirdly sort of partners.
The poor bedraggled thing, waiting all these dozing years!
I suppose I used to wonder if you could dicker and outwit
Your death, but now only wish I will have a chance to dig
It, you know what I mean? I don't mean this in a macabre
Way. It's more like your death is a part of your life, right?
I don't want to live companionably with it for a long time,
But it *will* be absorbing to get to know it a little before we
Wander off into the wilderness. As soon as I die my death
Does too, but who knows what happens to who *I* was? It's

Like this: I might get a whole new gig, as an otter or a bee,
Or a glowering angel assigned to protect a Uruguayan boy,
But old death expires like a yellowed coupon you discover
In a coat you last wore to church to pray, on All Souls Day.

You Know

Guy says to me last night, in the middle of the social ramble,
Can I tell you about my daughter? Yes? She struggled awful.
She did. We were terrified when we sent her away to college.
Her mother and me . . . we were scared. I kid you not. She did
Every drug you can do. Believe me I know them all now. I'd
Have to get one and google it to identify what she was taking
Too much of this time. It was a special sort of hell. Turns out
You can love someone and hate what they do, you surely can.
Fine line between that and hating *her*, though—very fine line.
That's all I wanted to tell you, that I was so near to hating my
Own child. It worked out. Something happened, and she's ok.
I guess a normal story would be how she came around, a kind
Of miracle or rebirth, and that's a great story, I'll tell you that
Story maybe, but today I just had to *say* it, that I was so close.
I was so close. The kid I begged God for I almost hated worse
Than I ever hated anyone in my whole life. Doesn't say much
For my character, I guess. But you have kids. *You* know. They
Drive you insane. You would do anything for them but there's
Times when you are awfully close to just hating your own kid.
This feels like confession. But you have kids—you know what
I mean. I just had to get it out. Now we can get back to regular
Talking. No one ever admits that. She's so much better. I wake
Up every morning scared, though, still. I suppose I always will.

Lent

One time I was trying to explain the concept of Lent
To my young twin sons. They were four years old &
Perfect and hilarious and headlong and extraordinary
In their genuineness, you know what I mean? Utterly
Unadorned, no agenda, didn't know how to lie, eager
For the next minute, but thoughtful, and already both
Reflective, as four-year-olds go; I heard them talking
One evening, in their beds, about their first memories.
But this time we were sprawled in the grass and I said
Well, Lent is a time of stripping away the usual things
And getting back to bones. Some people give up wine,
Or chocolate, or dessert, or television, to try to remind
Themselves that underneath fun is love and work, sort
Of. You know what I mean? No, they did not, and they
Happily spent a while thinking of the stuff they would
Give up, like beets, and brushing their teeth. Then one
Boy stood up and said if he was going to go to Lent he
Would give up clothes, which he then proceeded to do,
Followed by his brother, and they ran around laughing
So hard they no kidding fell down. Something snapped
Awake in me, something broke open. Sometimes there
Is a moment in life when something cuts through murk
And muddle and advice and bombast and opinionating,
Something just slices through all the burble and mutter,
Through the received and ostensible wisdom, the natter
And chatter, and reminds us why we are here. We name
This satori, epiphany, revelation—even this we have to

Find a label for, a handle to begin to understand it—but
It's not something a word can explain or define, or even
Really hint at, as far as provenance or effect. It *happens*,
And you see and hear and apprehend it, and we're agape
And rattled and thrilled and awed. It comes when it does.
You are lucky if it happens once, and blessed if there are
More than one in life. I got one that day on the lawn, yes
I did, and every year when Lent rolls around I remember
That naked lesson, so to speak, about what really matters
In this life—and now, I observe with a smile, so will you.